Life with Wine

Life with Wine

*A Self-Portrait of the Wine Business
in the Napa and Sonoma Valleys*

**Plus 100 Recipes
That Go with the Product**

Nancy Chirich

Drawings by John Simpkins

'ed-it
productions
Oakland, California

TO MAX and TO MILA, WITH LOVE.

Produced by 'ed-it
P.O. Box 29527
Oakland, California 94604

Manufactured in the United States of America.

3584

Editor: Gretchen Stengel
Indexer: Hilma S. Anderson
Proofreader: Barbara Dalton
Typeset by Cragmont Publications
Printed by Abbey Press, Inc.

Library of Congress Cataloging in Publication Data
Main entry under title:

Life with wine.

Includes bibliographical references and index.
1. Wine industry—California. 2. Wine and wine making—California. 3. Cookery, American—California. 4. Cookery (Wine) I. Chirich, Nancy. II. Simpkins, John, 1951-
HD9377. C2L53   1984   338.4'76632'00979419   83-16556
ISBN 0-912761-00-8

CONTENTS

Preface

When the idea for *"Life with Wine"* first came to us, we envisioned speaking with representatives of all the wineries in California.

Upon discovery that the sum total of these equals 460, we modified our ambitions to include only Northern California wineries, and then, the number still dismayingly large, modified them yet again, settling at last on a sampling from the Napa and Sonoma Valleys for insights into the industry as a whole.

As of early 1984, the production end of the business in the two valleys includes 83 wineries of all sizes from garage operations to giant corporations. Our sampling amounts to roughly 14.3 percent of the wineries within the Napa Valley appellation and 9.7 percent in that of the Sonoma Valley. While these figures might not impress a Gallup or Harris poll-taker, all of the interviewees quoted speak for some of their industry some of the time.

The format of this book is intended to show agreement as well as differences of opinion on certain issues important to the wine industry, such as would occur in informal conversation among colleagues. Our agreement not to cite the sources of individual quotes made for frankness in each intereview. Sources of information are listed in the Acknowledgments.

Acknowledgments

This book would not have been possible without the generous help and cooperation of those who live "Life with Wine". Sincere thanks and best wishes to:

Brother Timothy, Cellarmaster
The Christian Brothers Mont LaSalle Vineyards, Napa Valley

James Bundschu, President
Gundlach-Bundschu Winery, Sonoma Valley

Julia Garvey, Marketing Director
Flora Springs Winery, Napa Valley

Mr. and Mrs. Joseph E. Heitz
Heitz Wine Cellars, Napa Valley

Sandra and William MacIver, Owners
Matanzas Creek Winery, Sonoma Valley

Louis P. Martini, President
Louis M. Martini, Napa Valley

Scottie McKinney, Food & Wine Consultant
San Francisco

Myron S. Nightingale, Sr., Winemaker
Beringer Vineyards, Napa Valley

Charles Olken and Earl Singer
Connoisseur's Guide to California Wine
San Francisco

Cornelius S. Ough, Chairman
Department of Viticulture & Enology
University of California, Davis

Sebastian Titus and Wesley Poole
Titus & Poole Art and Design Studio, Napa

Very special thanks also to the individuals and wineries contributing the recipes in Part 2 of "Life with Wine."

Special thanks are also due the following, for sharing information, expertise, and/or moral support on the occasionally bumpy road of "Life":

Jean-Louis Brindamour, Strawberry Hill Press; Pauline McGuire and Fred Felder, Cragmont Publications; Virginia Jacobs, Buena Vista Vineyards; Margaret Mallory, Food Editor, *The Oakland Tribune*; Harvey Steiman, Food & Wine Editor, *The San Francisco Examiner*; Allan R. Mann and Bettis Shaw, Abbey Press, Inc.; Jack Mooradian, Laney Community College; Sandra Smires, American Viticultural Area Association, Guenoc Winery, Middletown, California; Jim Brandley, Trumpetvine Wines, Berkeley; The Wine Institute, San Francisco; Editor Gretchen Stengel, Indexer Hilma Sjolund Anderson, Proofreader Barbara Dalton, and Artists Raúl del Rio and John Simpkins; Rollin and Aida Anderson; and the research staffs of the Oakland Public Library and the Alameda County Business Library and of Bancroft Library at the University of California at Berkeley.

References

Magary, Alan, and Kerstin Fraser Magary. *Across the Golden Gate*. New York: Harper Colophon Books, Harper & Row. 1980.

Guide to California's Wine Country. 3rd Ed. Menlo Park, Calfornia: Lane Publishing Co. 1982.

Lichine, Alexis. *New Encyclopedia of Wines and Spirits*. 3rd Ed. New York: Knopf. 1981.

a gourmet picnic

1. Life with Wine

The Making of a Vintner

Life with wine!

In springtime, neat rows of vines march like sentinels amid bright flowers . . . . Before the autumn harvest, plump, juicy grapes glow like dusty jewels . . . .

The gentle laughter of light-hearted people, crystal glasses raised, floats on sunlit air . . . .

Who has never dreamed of life with wine, and the romance that must go with it?

But how does the dream come true?

This is a pretty good field for a young person to aim to get into. It's about the same as if you were going into food technology, a food processing plant, or just graduated as a chemist or a bacteriologist. It's right on par with those industries. There's a pretty good future, but they move around a lot. Once they get settled, a lot have ended up eventually owning their own places, getting started very small and then slowly growing.

I figure that the technologist that graduated from a university really couldn't run a winery on his own for the first five years. It would take somebody over him or a consultant that would come in regularly for at least the first five years, because there are so many things that happen in a plant that without a little bit of experience it would be very difficult to cope. If you didn't have somebody helping out, you can make an awful lot of mistakes — everything from spoiling wines to having equipment go out on you at a crucial point — something's happening all the time.

• • •

It's still rather a narrow field, which I think it takes a long time to really get ahead in, particularly if you're trying to make fine wines, and if you are sticking to basic principles and looking for long growth.

In most wineries if you go in as a winemaker, that's where you're going to wind up, unless you are an owner, or the son of the boss, or whatever. There are very few opportunities to go in as a winemaker and progress up the road as we used to know it in the big industrial plants — going up from winemaker to manager up to the presidency. Chances of that happening today are absolutely nil.

Oh sure, there are a lot of winemakers that have the title of vice president. I don't know whether that's to keep them from jumping and going to work somewhere else, or whatever.

On the other side of the coin, probably the popularity of wine and the interest we have in wine today from the young people is one of the reasons that a lot of new wineries have opened up, and that gives an opportunity for people to get in, with more jobs available. But there are probably very few wineries in the state that have more than six or seven in the executive office. You find a lot of trained technicians and mechanics.

Sometimes some of us are prone to think that here's a great romance and we're going to turn the corner in two or three years, without realizing that it takes a minimum of, I think, ten years to turn the corner.

• • •

Some people are going into the wine business as a livelihood for their families, but by far most of the new wineries, I'm sure, have an outside income of some sort, either from another business or from an inheritance or something, because they're simply not big enough to really make a living at it yet. They'll keep growing, sure they will, but if you start a new winery, it should take you about ten years to get into the black, where you start making some money at it. You've gotta have pretty darn good resources to start with.

• • •

You don't necessarily have to have a lot of money.

There's still some room for the very small efforts — that would be garage efforts. But they have to make an *excellent* wine, not just a good wine. The wines have to be the best in their class. Therefore, the collectors will seek them out and they can get good prices and make a profit.

• • •

Back in the '70s it was very easy, and many people did just start wineries for the love of making wine. They could start making their wine in a garage and selling 500 cases to be able to make a thousand cases next year. That was definitely easily attained with dedication, but today with the marketing situation and the number of California wines, and also Oregonian and Washingtonian, and Italian, French, Chilean, Hungarian, Bulgarian, it's still just as easy to make your wine in your garage, but it's far more difficult to market it and to sell 500 cases of wine to finance 1000 cases of wine the next vintage. So in that vein it has changed to where today it is more likely that to get started in a winery you want to have a tremendous amount of capital from an outside source, or to inherit. Those are really the only two avenues.

That's not to say that there still aren't some people who are starting in their garages, which is great because they're a colorful segment of the wine business and it should never be an industry which excludes people who want to make a better bottle of wine, because that's what progress is. It's just far more difficult to do that now.

• • •

Our winemaker has a great reputation. She has been called "the true Burgundian". She had come up to take a job and the deal fell through. My wife brought her next door to the old dairy barn here and said "Do you think you could make wine in this place? Can we renovate it?"

She said "No way!" But we finally convinced her we could change the pigeon roof and get another row of barrels.

It just had to work, so we made it work. We didn't know anything about winemaking — in fact, not much about wine. We just like the great out-of-doors, a business that will allow country living.

It was because our winemaker was around that the winery began. If you have grapes and you have a place where you can make wine and there's a Merry Edwards around, you don't let her slip by. You just jump and say, "Well, we hadn't planned doing this yet, but ... ."

• • •

It's been very fortunate for us, because in this case my dad owns this land, he owns this building, and the partnership — my two brothers and their wives, Mom and Dad and my husband and I — rents the building from him, so that's an advantage. If we were just going to start and we had to build a building, it would put us in the hole.

This property had fallen into decay and my father bought it as a retirement and investment project. It was during a drought year. The vines were all dried up, and everything looked awful. He had no idea that the children would be interested in it, but we fell in love with it.

Then my brother came up also, and there was another old building on the property, and he completely renovated that and made it into his home. He commutes into Berkeley on a daily basis. He said if I'm going to be nuts enough to do this commuting, we've got this building here, let's at least make a little bit of wine for fun. So that's basically the way we started. We've made it into a much larger project than my father had anticipated, or probably would have been able to do.

Our background's not in wine, but we've been like sponges since we moved up here, absorbing every piece of knowledge we can on wines and on grape growing and on making wine. My husband worked with a fellow who is extremely knowledgeable about vineyards who was like a tutor for over a year. They worked hand in hand together, and little by little he weaned himself away. It's gotten to the point where people call him now and ask for advice on managing their vineyards, so I think we've been successful in absorbing knowledge and putting it to work.

• • •

It was just purely "Gee, that looks like a nice thing to do — why don't we try that?" And the next thing we knew, we were digging holes and planting vines.

Neither of us does any planting any more. We're chained to those desks these days. We worked in the vineyard until last year. The year before, we had the assistant winemaker handling sales and the winemaker making the wine. That's when we picked up and realized in retrospect — to put it in the terminology that we got from the accountant — we had the product, but we didn't have the business end tied up. So we put the winemaker in charge of the vineyards, and we started taking over sales, marketing, the business end completely ourselves.

● ● ●

Just like my son who's working down there now, I started working on vacations on the ranch. Having grown up in the business, my father and I felt there was no need for me to go to Davis. Besides, he was second generation going to Berkeley and he wanted to have a third generation, so that's where I went to school. I studied Economics there and that was very valuable, especially today.

I had a good foundation in growing grapes just living it all my life, so I wanted to get away and go into some other field, just to see what the rest of the world had to offer, because I'd always been sequestered here on the ranch. While I was in the Coast Guard I went to night school and obtained a real estate license. That lasted six months and then I came back to farming. It didn't take me long to find out how lucky I was.

The Romantic Life

Winemakers themselves seem to believe that wine as a way of life is not very romantic.

Be that as it may, most of the interviews took place in charming surroundings — here in the shade of great blooming camellias, there on a veranda of worn stone facing long vineyard vistas that disappeared into the blue mist of towering mountains. And always, the heady sparkle of wine was in the air.

To me this industry has always been very attractive and it's been a wonderful life for me. I never became a millionaire, but I've been exposed to an awful lot of different things, and met a lot of fantastic personalities, and it's given me the opportunity to travel all over the world. I've seen all segments of it from one end to the other — concentrate, brandy production, hybrid production, dessert wines — and all these things have been very interesting to me.

The glamor of it started the first day I walked into the winery, because otherwise I don't think I'd have stood it this long. But how do you compare the wine business with canned pumpkin or canned peas?

• • •

I've always been attracted to the wine business. Driving around, looking at what a beautiful area you can live in, and the way of life — the romantic life — got me. Of course, we all laugh about it in the industry — what a romantic job we have! But that quickly disappears. You work so hard at the same things over and over and over again it defeats romanticism. It's familiarity also. After awhile, in anyone's job, no matter what it appears to be from the outside, there's not so much mystique once you're involved in it. It's nuts and bolts, like anything else. The romantic side dissipates into you've got to have a new pump, or the tractor transmission has gone out, which are two immediate problems we're having.

• • •

When you're in business for yourself, there's a tremendous amount of stress that you put on yourself. If you work for someone else and you lose your job, there's stress because you depend on that money to support your family. But when you have your own business you have so much more to lose. You've invested not only your time and your effort, but you also may have hocked yourself up to the hilt to get established.

I think this business is comprised of a lot of over-achievers. At least the people I know are in here not because it's a romantic industry, because that certainly burns off right away. We're in here because we want to succeed at this, and we're building something not just for ourselves but for our children, and so there's a lot of tension in that.

For many people in *this* (the Napa) valley, this is a second or third career. They have been successful in other businesses and they don't want to be anything less than successful. I see people who've had some *really* successful careers as attorneys and accountants and so on, and they're out there at one o'clock in the morning turning on their frost machines, and working long, long, long hours, and putting every bit of their blood and guts into it. In that sense it's stressful. It's not stressful like if you go into an office, and you're closed in and your stress is because someone's imposed a job on you that maybe you don't want. We just went to a party down the Peninsula and saw a bunch of friends that we've known from years ago and they maybe have more stress than us, in that they're not happy in their jobs, but I would say we work much harder than they do.

• • •

You don't feel deadlines and pressure. Not if you run things right. You're pretty tied to Nature. If you wait till the day before the grapes get ripe to get the crushers ready, then you're under stress, but you've got all summer to do it in, so by the time the grapes get ripe if you're ready to go, there's no pressure. A lot of pressure is created by individuals in many jobs, as far as that goes. The printing industry is one of the worst ones. They always wait till the last minute to deliver labels or whatever we get made. I've never seen any of them come in ahead of time.

It's interesting, but not exotic. It's not particularly hard work, or unpleasant, like someone working in a steel plant that's got a furnace right in front of his face or something like that, but it's still just plain everyday labor. You pull hoses around, or clean tanks, or move barrels, and do a lot of these things that are just plain work. As far as the people actually in the winery doing the work, it isn't all that romantic, and nothing can be more boring than the girls standing on the bottling line putting capsules on the bottles as they come by.

• • •

I'm sure in the big corporations they're out beating their head on the wall as though they were selling steel or automobiles, so sure, it's stressful. But the smaller wineries like this have never been greedy, have been willing to go slowly. I want to make a decent living but I don't want to drive anybody else out of business doing it. In a small valley such as this, we're neighbors. We party together, the kids go to school together, and a lot of them go to the same church. If somebody runs out of glue or somebody runs out of foils or something we trade back and forth. If somebody has a problem, they'll go to a neighbor for help. Or if a problem pops up in *a* winery that could spread to everyone, we'll call a meeting and try to stop that problem before it spreads.

It's certainly an industry where people work well with each other. Robert Mondavi once made a statement that I quote frequently: "We're in competition *with* each other, we're not in competition against each other." And that's a big difference. It's a *good* business to work in, because people basically like each other.

They're kind of the same type — basically farmers, but evolved from that quite a bit in different ways. Some of the new people, the ex-stockbrokers, ex-lawyers, are basically the same too. That's one reason why they came. They see this sort of life. They would like to be part of it. So most of them try to adjust. Like in any world made up of little circles, there's always going to be a poop here and there . . . .

• • •

This industry shares more than any I've ever seen. Even schoolteachers don't share information like I see vineyardists and winemakers do. I think it's because ultimately you're dealt certain cards and you've got to play with them. So even though so-and-so may give you their little secrets of how they made wine last year, it might not work for your grapes, so what harm is there in sharing? There's a vintner's group and there's an ag group, and you go to the meetings and you talk to people and say I'm having trouble with . . . mealyworms. Do you know somebody who knows about them? And sometimes the answer is right there.

What would we be doing now if we weren't in the wine business is a good question. I really don't know. Because there are times when my husband and I get really tired, and we feel like we've been running in opposite directions for days on end, and even though we live together and work together, there's times we don't feel we have that quality time together, because I'm running off and doing a tasting on a Sunday, which is his only day off .... And we ask ourselves, are we going to do this *forever?* This is the pits! And then we sit down and we cannot think of anything we'd rather do. This gets into your blood. It's an extension of us. And even though we gripe and groan sometimes, I don't think we'd find anything we'd enjoy as much.

One of our big fears when we moved up here from the city was that we would be bored. We just laugh at that now, because there just aren't enough hours in the day to get everything done. We're so lucky. We really are.

• • •

There's none of us in the business for our health, I don't think. We can talk about romance and all that, but it's still a hard-nosed business. But where else can you go to a country club and work?

• • •

It's definitely hectic sometimes, but stress is eliminated by the product you're dealing with. It's awfully difficult to built up stress when you're consistently drinking wine and dining with interesting people. And that's basically what the wine business is. It's growing the best grapes you possibly can out in the field, and then relaxing. You have to work like any other job, but you're outside with Mother Nature on a nice day like today .... And in the four walls of the winery you're making wine, which is a beautiful product. And then in order to sell it, you're constantly tasting wine with people and dining with them to show them how wine goes with food. We do have to get out of bed every morning and go to work, and work all day long, but it's not a stressful occupation.

It seems very romantic, and that attracts a lot of people to the industry. When the romance is steamed off, there's just a lot of hard work involved. But sitting on a tractor seat on a day like today is romantic to me, so — it all depends on your interpretation of the word.

The Vineyard

Winemaker and grape grower are sometimes one and the same. If not, the problems are still mutual, for the ultimate goal of both is the best wine possible, with Nature, of course, the final arbiter of which grapes will be among the chosen.

Growing Grapes

Grape growers are just like any other farmer — a very independent lot of individuals. The closest tie that a grower has is to the winery that he's selling his grapes to, because they're in a unified partnership. The grower must grow the finest grapes for the winery to produce the finest wines, so the grower's affiliation is foremost with the winery. There are other entities such as Sonoma County and Napa Valley Grape Growers Associations where you get together once a month and meet and have a technical dissertation on pruning methods or trellising methods or new equipment available, but mostly those are social organizations, and there's no union per se.

Many wineries — particularly the larger wineries — have their own vineyards and also purchase many grapes because they are so large. Many small wineries don't have the capital to both grow grapes and produce wine. Most small quote "estate" wineries purchase their grapes from growers.

It varies from vintage to vintage, but predominantly about 70 percent of the wine that we produce is estate-bottled from grapes that we grow right around the winery. We do buy from a couple of neighbors. About 20 percent of our production in the winery is purchased from other growers, and we sell about 30 percent of our grapes to other wineries, so we're constantly playing back and forth.

As a grower, it's just facing Mother Nature. This year has been a very wet year. Some years are very dry. You compensate in the field as best you can. The vines dictate, and you always want to treat the vines the best that they possibly can be treated. If they don't have enough moisture then you compensate by pruning differently and being much more aware of the weeds in the vineyard. You garden better, that's what it amounts to as a grower.

• • •

The wineries want the fruit properly ripe. They want

the acidity to be correct on it, and they don't want too many grapes put on the vine so it's overcropped. They want a reasonable crop of grapes on the vine, they don't want the grapes to be moldy, and they want them picked and brought in the same day.

There's a lot of little problems that arise that are sometimes written into contracts. For a certain percent sugar grape, they'll pay so much money, in range for anything over or less than that, they'll pay less. If there's so much mold or rot in the grapes they decrease the price. Beyond a certain limit they'll reject the load and won't buy at all. These are always problems — economic problems. The farmer, he's got the grapes and he wants to sell them. The winery won't buy them unless they make good wine.

Right now there's the third-party inspection system set up in California. It's monitored by the State Department of Agriculture, and they train people to sample odd loads to determine the percentage of sugar and also the amount of rot in there, if that's requested. This has been paid for in the past by the winery, but now there's a question if this should be a joint payment by both winery and grower, because the growers request it. They really want this because they think the wineries cheat them. The wineries have a real problem convincing the farmer that they're being fair about this. They have economic restrictions and things in selling their wine.

Like last year, for example, was the biggest crop of grapes we've ever had in California and the winery sales were down. They couldn't possibly handle all the grapes —there was no place to put them once they had them, so they were rather arbitrary in some instances on rejecting some loads, and saying we're going to distill these instead of making wine out of them. It caused some problems among wineries and grape growers, but it's a minor problem in the long run.

● ● ●

We grow about 65 percent of our grapes and purchase

the other. We buy from several growers around here and in Sonoma County primarily. Most of them are small, 40-50-100 acres or something like that. They usually come around when they have something to sell. We've had the same ones now for quite a number of years. So every year we just take whatever they produce. They know they can bring it here, unless . . .

If we do eliminate a grower, like we eliminated this last year because we just had too many grapes, we simply write to them early in the year like in January and tell them that we're sorry that this year we can't take their grapes, and that gives them nine months practically to find a home for them.

The growers are in a more tense economic situation from year to year than a winery because they can't hold their product. But there's a limit to how long a winery can hold it too. First of all, the product doesn't stand holding that long in bulk, but secondly it's expensive to put in a cooperage for inventories that you're not going to move. Pretty soon you run out of space.

• • •

We grow somewhere in the neighborhood of 85 to 95 percent of our needs. The only grapes we're buying right now are those grapes we are actually short on ourselves, and in a few years we will have vineyards for those — Chenin Blanc, some French Colombard, and a little Sauvignon Blanc. But all the Chardonnay we grow ourselves, Cabernet . . . with the exception of a little block over there on a private vineyard on a ranch. We grow our own grapes. We've got control of the grapes out there.

I don't necessarily mean to infer that if you're buying grapes you cannot have as good control, because in today's market you can tell the grower just about anything you want, and that's the way it's going to be if he wants to sell the grapes.

There are a lot of vineyardists releasing a lot of growers today because of surpluses. It makes it very easy for the winemaker if you are growing most of your grapes. You feel a lot freer.

Some Vineyard Enemies

Coping with a variety of pests is the lot of every farmer. A vineyard is host to several natural enemies. Even phylloxera, which once had a cataclysmic impact on the wine industry world-wide, is still around.

The cleanup of virus in the stalk is by far the most important advance from a winemaking point of view as well as from a grape-growing point of view. It gives the wineries good, clean, better quality fruit to start with.

Phylloxera is an insect — a plant louse, and Pierce's is a bacterial infection. Virus is another thing, carried by nematodes, some of them, or transferred from vine to vine by cutting and grafting.

The way it's eliminated is by growing the plants in very warm conditions in a hothouse, hot enough so the vines are just barely able to stay alive, and the viruses don't move into the new tips of the shoots as the vine slowly grows. The tips are generally clean of virus and they snip those tips off and culture those into new plants that are free of the virus. And they have what they call plant indicators where they graft those new plants onto plants that show a virus response by some change in their growing habits or appearance, and they detect if they are still virus-infected or not.

• • •

Phylloxera, an insect that lives in the soil and eats the roots of grapevines, swept the North Coast area through the Napa Valley from about 1880 to about 1900, and was pronouncedly bad about 1890. The same bug happened to hit Europe at almost the same time and went through Western Europe.

This little bug originates apparently somewhere in the Americas, maybe in North America. It was transported across the Atlantic to western Europe without anybody being aware that it had been transported. I think it was first discovered in one of these graperies, a kind of a hothouse in which they grew grapes in England, or it might have been in connection with an agricultural research station in England. I think it was 20 years later or so that they recognized that it was also to be found in vineyards in France.

It's a little thing — not fully microscopic. That is, if you have it on a clean white piece of paper you can see it with your naked eye, but you need a microscope or some kind of a lens if you want to count the legs or see really what it looks like. You can understand how it would be difficult for a farmer to see it in the dirt or on the roots of the vines, or to understand what it was.

We do have phylloxera all through the county and just about everybody plants on a native American rootstock that has some resistence to this phylloxera bug. The University of California at Davis is our best source of good new material. They propagate things and turn them over to nurseries to be multiplied. We work with nurseries that work in close conjunction with the University.

At the surface of the soil we bud or graft on the desired grape variety we want above the ground. Each grapevine that you see out in the vineyard has a certain kind of rootstock, and has a different kind of material growing above the ground level. And this is true in most of western Europe as well as along the north coast here and in much of California.

We have some areas of California where the phylloxera bug has never really gotten a foothold — in light sandy soils the phylloxera are hardly there at all. But in soils that have more loam or clay, where the soils will have more cracks when it shrinks in the summer and the soil changes consistency from wet to dry, the phylloxera live much more than in the light sandy soil. Bale gravelly loam is one of the principal soils of the floor of the Napa Valley. Up in the hills, there's a lot of volcanic gravel.

We know the bug is there, we know we can fumigate the soil, we can kill, say, a million phylloxera per acre or something like that but there might be a few hundred of them that we have not been able to kill. Well, over a period of time they'll propagate, and you'll have more of them than you had before.

You can't fumigate your land every year because grapevines are perennial — you want that grapevine to live and produce fruit for you for a number of years. So to fumigate and kill the phylloxera we use a gas that we inject in the soil. But it'll also kill the grapevine, so the land has to be cleaned.

We have to have all of the grapevines pulled out and most of the roots and a lot of the rocks removed, and we have to have the land worked up so we can pull the proper tillage instrument with little injector tubes to inject the poison gas down in the soil through the vineyard and smooth over the dirt behind the machine to seal the surface a bit so the gas doesn't escape right away. We're not absolutely sure how deep that gas penetrates in a given piece of soil, nor how deep the phylloxera might be in a given piece of soil, so we can never do an absolutely 100 percent perfect job, but we do the best we can.

Then we plant vines again in that fumigated soil and hope they will produce grapes for 30 years, 40 years, 50 years — until we have to pull them out and fumigate again.

If we didn't have disease organisms and parasites like the phylloxera to fight, the grapevine could live a couple of hundred years.

An Interview with:

The Chairman of the Department of Viticulture and Enology University of California, Davis

The sprawling campus of the University of California at Davis, near the lush, flat heart of the Sacramento River Delta, remains almost as bucolic as in 1905, when it began as the University Farm. The rural atmosphere, however, has not hindered its international reputation among winemakers.

The Department of Viticulture and Enology is crowded along with other science departments into the three stories of Wickson Hall, a relatively new and hideous building that appears to be bursting its seams. Enrollment in Viticulture and Enology increased four to five times in the '60s and '70s, keeping pace with worldwide interest in and consumption of wine.

Students receive a degree in either Enology, the laboratory side of winemaking, or Viticulture, the agricultural side. From Davis they can go into other fields such as brewing or general food science, but the majority go into wineries, not just in California, but all over the world. Most of the foreign students go home to work — to South Africa, Australia, France, Germany, and Italy — for the wine industry is expanding everywhere. Members of the faculty often travel abroad in an academic capacity. Professor Emeritus Maynard Amerine, for example, has been a guest researcher at the Magarach Research Institute at Yalta ["the Napa Valley of the Soviet Union"], one of the oldest centers of enology in the world.

Since before its gradual evolution from the Department of Viticulture and Fruit Products at U.C. Berkeley to its official opening in the early fifties as the Department of Viticulture and Enology at U.C. Davis, the Department has aided and abetted the wine industry of California. A Department expert is usually available for consultation, often in the field; U.S. Department of Agriculture Extension Service Bulletins are derived from the field work and research of both the U.S.D.A. and the Department; and recently it began a program of all-day short courses for people in the industry. One such seminar treats the analysis of wine for sugar, copper and iron content; another covers the latest scientific findings in table wine processing.

While it is not the only school to provide respectable credentials for winemaking — many graduates in Enology of the California State University at Fresno, for instance, work in the wineries of the Napa and Sonoma Valleys — because of proximity, the Department of Viticulture and Enology at U.C. Davis seems part and parcel of the wine industry of the North Coast.

Professor Cornelius S. Ough [pronounced "O"], a tall, handsome man on the silver side of 50 who resembles a shrewd Dutch uncle, is Chairman of the Department.

When I came here in 1950 there weren't that many wineries in California. A class of 10 was immense. At least half were foreign students, and otherwise mostly sons of winery people. Now the undergraduate enrollment is 150 in Enology, with 40 in Viticulture — rather a lot for us. The Department was not designed to handle that many.

One reason I think this Department's had a reasonable amount of success is that we are a joint department. The quality of the grape is what regulates the quality of the wine. It's old-hat to say it, but it's very true. You can't make good wine out of poor grapes. You can make bad wine out of good grapes, but to make good wine, you need the good grapes to make it. There's just no exception to that rule.

We have a good understanding with the industry I think. They appreciate what we do, and we try to support them as much as we can in our research areas. For instance, Sebastiani gives $12,000 — not a scholarship, but a research assistanceship. Part of that money goes to support the student, part goes for new equipment, new material and things for the student's research. And then the Monterey Wine Festival gave us $10,000 last year as scholarships. Those are pretty healthy funds to get research established.

A donor can't direct the research, but they can say they'd like to have the work in certain areas, and we certainly make all efforts to do that. The University doesn't accept gifts with strings attached.

It's a very dramatic thing to see the changes in the vineyards in California in the last 30 years. I got into it when it was just starting to improve, and there have been some really dramatic changes in the technology.

It's very difficult in the scientific world to take credit for any one thing, so it can't be said that a lot of technical changes are due to U.C. Davis. There's a lot of literature in the world on winemaking. In the University you read it all, and when you see something that catches your eye you may do experiments and see that it works and then you promote it.

That's essentially what happened when the realization dawned that temperature control is the most important factor in making white wine. It wasn't originated in any university, but we recognized the importance of it and pushed it in California. The industry here was one of the first to buy lots of refrigeration and control the temperature and make better, fruitier white wine.

That's why the white wine market took off. The wines were fresh and fruity and people liked them and drank them. Even after World War II white wines were generally not very good — sort of oxydized when they'd been around a long time — not fruity and nice and clean like they are now.

The vines in the past have contained various viruses. This was recognized here probably first by Professor Emeritus Harold Olmo, and then by Professor Goheen, a Plant Pathology U.S.D.A. employe. With others, they eventually set up the Foundation Plant Material Program here and learned how to remove the virus from the vines.

I do a certain amount of travelling around the world in

areas where they still haven't completely cleaned their vineyards up. You see a clean vineyard — every vine growing equally well, and vigorous. Then you see these other vineyards — the virus-infested stalk still there. There may be a medium-good vine among the weak, but never a full growth and the vineyard looks terrible. That's how ours used to look. I can remember.

Dr. Olmo was doing clonal work before World War II, so I'd say right after the war they got started. He went out and searched the whole state for the best, healthiest vines, and saw immediately there were some areas where the vines were very healthy and then the same variety would be completely weak. The leaves would curl up on them, and the fruit didn't get ripe — for no good reason. He brought them all to one location, and things didn't change any. So location wasn't to blame. Virus infestation was.

The Department of Viticulture and Enology has several programs in progress, all of which are highly important to California's wine industry.

On the enological side, there is ongoing research on yeast fermentation problems, wine stability during aging and storage, color extraction, organic constituents, malo-lactic fermentation, sensory evaluation [what compounds give what odors to wine], gasohol, and, with U.C. Medical School, on allergic reactions to sulphur dioxide, which has been added to wine since recorded history to help inhibit bacteria that might grow in the barrels.

There's always challenges in this business. One thing is to develop better yeasts so we can modify the flavor of wine with yeast rather than just having to depend on the grapes. It's much easier to genetically change yeast than it is to genetically change the plants, and the system is well on its way to being perfected now. Right now we're trying to get a new faculty member to work in this area. We feel it's a tremendously important one for the industry.

In Viticulture, the nutritional aspects of the grape, including the effects of irrigation, are being studied, and at the Kearney Field Station the physiology of the grape, how it grows, the effect of sunlight, photosynthesis on table grapes.

Professor Meredith, a geneticist, has lots of support from the industry in her work on the clonal selections by individual cells — the cloning of vines. What she does is disrupt the material down to the cellular form and then put that on agriplates where there is some compound that may inhibit the growth, or may not — a high salt, for example — and see if any of the cells have mutated enough to grow against the salt barrier that's there. If they do, she hopes to eventually take that cell and grow a plant from it.

What will happen is the cell will grow like any other culture and form a little mound that can be grown eventually into a full-sized plant, hopefully to carry that resistance against the salt, and can be planted in any climate where previously it couldn't be grown.

A grape generation is from three to five years. In the past the way plants have been selected is you make a bunch of seedling crosses and plant them and see how resistant they are, and this takes *years*. First you have to pollinate the plant, gather the seeds, generate small plants — get big plants and so on.

These are *different* plants — they're not the same as the mother plant. A clone is the same material, basically the same plant. You make clones of Cabernet Sauvignon grapes, it's still Cabernet Sauvignon, with maybe one or two different features, but maybe not even that. But if you make crosses, they're completely different — may turn out to be white grapes instead of red — may not taste like Cabernet Sauvignon or anything else. So this is a controlled way to go about this selection of resistent material . . . .

I've had lots of good years in the industry. It's all been an enjoyable challenge in an enjoyable field . . . . An enjoyable time.

Winemaking

Winemaking defies neat categorization. Besides technology, such imponderables as creative talent, luck, and Nature are all part of the production process.

A Delicate Balance

Wine is both an art and a science, and there's a lot to learn about both sides of it.

• • •

You distinguish a great wine by what it does to you when you taste it. If it makes you want to stand up and cheer and say "My, this is *wonderful* stuff!" then it's a great wine. It's art. What's the difference between Vladimir Horowitz and another pianist who may be a music student? The student may play all the notes better than Horowitz — maybe more technically perfect than Horowitz — but it doesn't get you in the gut the way Horowitz' playing does. Chateau Margaux is not a perfect wine every year, but it gets you because it's a wonderful wine. You may find a technically more perfect *vin ordinaire*, but it's an ordinary wine. It doesn't have all the complexity and wonderful things.

• • •

The wine flavor is really supposed to come from the grape. Some people like an oaky wine, so they put them in new casks to get a strong oak character in it. But that's not really part of the wine flavor, it's something that has been added. The wine flavor itself comes from the variety of grape that you have. And a little bit on how you process it.

As far as wine *quality* goes, the most important thing that has happened in the last ten years is the planting of a lot of good grapes. Until you have the grapes, you can have all the technology in the world, but you're still not going to make good wines. Once you've got good grapes, the technology becomes more important, because then you've got the raw material with which to make a good wine. That to me is the most important advancement that's been done in the industry.

• • •

Wine is *not* manufactured. Wine is, let's say generated by the little living yeast cells that ferment the grape sugars into the grape alcohol of the wine. Wine is just fermented grape juice, so it's a natural process that these little living creatures of the Lord convert the grape juice into wine. You'll get a better wine if you give them the proper environment and the proper temperature in which to work, so we do a little gentle guidance, a little supervision, a little bit of baby-sitting of those yeast cells and the fermentation of the wine, but not much more than that.

You could say the wine makes itself, but we do add some cultured yeast cells so that we have a predictable product, rather than depend entirely upon the wild yeasts that are on the skins of the grape out in the vineyard, which may produce a rather unpredictable wine because we don't know exactly what yeast cells are on them.

The yeast cell itself is a little thing on the borderline between being a plant and an animal. I don't know if it's fully defined yet as either, so it's right about at no-man's land. But it multiplies itself, and converts your grape sugars into the grape alcohol of the wine.

• • •

We don't filter and refine our wines more than absolutely necessary. All of our red wines have sediment, all of our white wines have tartaric crystals — tartaric acid. When wine gets to a certain temperature, the cold will make the tartaric acid precipitate out into crystals. We get more corks in the mail — people sending us back pieces of "glass" when it's really crystals.

In order to get rid of those tartaric crystals, you have to super-cool the wines so they all drop out at the winery. Any time you do any of those operations to the wine, you strip some flavor from the wine. It's just inevitable.

It's sort of a rule for us that we don't strip wines of that extra flavor. I quote Professor Maynard Amerine frequently that this does *violence* to the wine, which I think is a great phrase.

The consumer can deal with a little bit of sediment, and should learn to. Actually crystals are the easiest thing to avoid, because they're heavy and sit at the bottom, and you can just drink down to it and they just stay there. All of us can live with a little something in the bottom of the glass. It makes a better wine.

Research and Development

As in all businesses that depend on meeting the demands of the consumer in a competitive market, constant research and development is essential in the wine industry.   From the smallest boutique winery to the largest corporate operation, "R & D" is an ongoing commitment.

Even in the winery we have consultants that come in, just because there's a fear and a reality that you become cellar-blind — that's what they call it. You've tasted your wines so many times that you like it, and you can't really look at it objectively. We have a man who consults for several wineries come in periodically and sit down and taste the wines with our winemaker because he can be objective. He doesn't taste it every day, or even every week. Then he'll say, "It seems to me you ought to be pulling this out of the barrels pretty soon," whereas the winemaker may be saying "I think it needs a little more time." Well, at least it makes us think about whether we should be making a move or not.

• • •

First we test the wine all by itself. In our laboratory we taste the wine as it is and we may do a little blending if we want to change something. We cleanse the palate with some unsalted crackers or a little bit of French bread and maybe rinse the mouth with water. We don't experiment with food in the wine laboratory or in the tasting lab. We don't want the extraneous smells of the foods in that room.

But then when it comes to the usage of wine during our own mealtime when we're eating, then we will experiment with our different wines to see how they go with the food. We'll do that in a dining room setting with the foods that happen to be available to us that day.

• • •

We do lots of tastings within our family, tasting our wines against our other wines and tasting other people's wines, and of course part of life up here is entertaining. If you're entertaining you certainly have wine with the meal. You start to get a feel for what goes well, and what doesn't go well, with certain foods.

• • •

We do a certain amount of . . . product research, if you like a name like that. We're always examining and reexamining things to see if we can improve something, or to see if there is something we can do that we've never done before that might result in a completely new product.

Let's say if we have a grape that produces a very nice, pleasant wine and we like it ourselves, we may decide OK, that's good. We like it, so there must be a lot of other people like us who would also like it. It ought to have a market. And so we'll put it on the market either with the grape varietal name or we may put it on the market with a proprietary name, some name that is not identified exactly with the grape variety.

One of the products that we developed and put on the market is our Chateau La Salle. It's our biggest selling wine at the moment. This is a light sweet wine that in terms of alcohol strength classifies with the table wines, but in terms of sweetness classifies as a dessert wine because it contains more that 10 percent residual grape sugar. That's pretty sweet.

It isn't highly alcoholic, but it goes very well with desserts and with between-meal snacks of various kinds and so it has popularity.

Another reason it may be our largest-selling wine would be that there's almost no other winery that has anything that is real close to it in style or character or quality. It sits out there in the wine market almost all by itself without a lot of competition. It would be different with something else like Chardonnay or Cabernet Sauvignon where lots of wineries are producing the very same line with the very same varietal name on the bottle. The Chardonnay and the Cabernet Sauvignon out in the marketplace do face a lot of competition on the shelves.

• • •

We are always working with different varieties grown in different areas. That's something we do on a continuing basis. We just bought a piece of land up in Lake County and we're going to start planting some of that with maybe a number of different varieties and see how they do. We're trying a new hybrid that the University has put out called "Carmine" at our Healdsburg ranch. This type of thing is on-going. Every year we've got something we're playing with. The public never sees it, because it's just small quantities to start with and ends up getting thrown into something else.

We are also doing quite a bit of experimenting with Pinot Noir and Merlot and some of the other varieties on skin contact times during fermentation, inclusion of stems in the fermentation ... a whole bunch of these little things. We keep that wine separate, and then evaluate it — let it age and taste it and decide if it's a good process and we'd like to pursue it and blend it with regular wine by normal technique, or change completely to that technique for producing it. We've done that from time to time — just change our method, because we've found a little bit better way of handling the wine.

But the small quantities we just evaluate. Then

eventually if we find that that's the way we'd like to do it, we go on and do the whole works.

We don't have an official panel other than ourselves — my son, who is doing most of the winemaking now, and I, and another fellow in the lab who does a lot of the analytical work and so on. We taste it and see what we think. It's always a comparison with something else. We point out why it's better, how we should maybe change. More often than that, we say, well, that's good but supposing we did things a little bit different? And we discuss that. Then if we feel it's worthwhile, then maybe next year come harvest-time, we'll try it. This goes on in all wineries, perhaps all the time.

When we get to the final blend quite often we bring some home to have with food to see how it goes. In the interim, when we're just trying some new process, no, because we've been doing this for so long now that we can pretty well correlate what the wine tastes like without the food and what the wine's going to taste like with food.

• • •

Our 300 acres of vineyard are not contiguous. They're located in various spots in the Valley. That means we have Chardonnay growing in three different locations. So we will bring in some Chardonnay from each location, and we'll keep them separate as long as possible. We'll ferment them differently. We'll use different types of barrels, different types of yeast, and we'll just experiment. What we're trying to do is to find out — now the Chardonnay that grows on this vineyard, how is it best made into a wine? Is it best completely barrel-fermented with this type of yeast, or is it best partially barrel-fermented or is it best stainless-steel fermented? And so what we end up with is 14 or 16 different wines, depending on how many experiments we do, and we taste them.

We know what the style that we want to make is, but we don't want to impose our style on the vineyard if that vineyard can't produce the style we want to make. We want to work hand in hand with what the vineyard best does and with what our hopes are. We may find that the wine that comes from this vineyard is really best done in this style. Now is this compatible with the style that we want to make? If it isn't, then we'll sell those grapes to someone else who may want to make it in that style. We're not surprised at the end of fermentation each year as to what our product is, because we've done our homework. We're not going to say "Oh this is a real disaster wine!" We kind of know what that vineyard is going to produce anyway, and if it is less than what we think it is, we'll sell it off. We'll bulk it out. You can't afford to put a less than good wine on the market right now.

● ● ●

We have several ways of testing new wine. We present it with the food here at home. Or, since we sell much of our wine to restaurants, we actually dine in the restaurant with the proprietor or chef and let them taste our wine with the food. It's just a constant education on both sides. There's a new upsurge of people wanting to know what food goes with what wine and vice versa, so there's becoming more affiliation with great chefs and great winemakers, because that is the end product — a meal with wine.

A Wine's Style

The grape determines the variety of wine, but wine from each variety can be made in several different styles — from an early or a late harvest, aged in oak from France or oak from Yugoslavia ... and so on. Guided by Nature, as usual, the winemaker determines a wine's style.

Style is a winemaking decision. The winemaker has to decide the style of wines to make and that should be in conversations with what the marketing people tell him.

Nowadays that is especially critical because the only thing a small winery can do is try and differentiate themselves from their competition. Outside of just marketing the name and so forth, that's pretty much all they can do. Because if you're making a wine just like the guy down the street . . . .

• • •

What we're trying to do is make a wine that when we release it you can be pleased to drink it, but will also give you great cellaring rewards. In other words, we're not trying to make a wine that you'd better drink in the next three months. At the same time we want to give you wine that you *can* drink in the next three months, but will even be better if you put it away for a little while. Some people, I think, try to make a wine that is *huge* and you just hope you live long enough so that you can enjoy it. Our wines, I would say, could be defined as being understated rather than overstated.

• • •

What you have to do is be specific and look at each variety of grape, and make a determination as to whether it can improve with aging in a bottle or whether aging really doesn't benefit the taste of the wine. You break it down on a variety basis.

Regarding bottle aging, we make a Riesling and Kleinberger that need to be consumed a year or two after they're bottled. The Chardonnay can age five to seven years. If someone has a baby and they want to serve the wine on the baby's 21st birthday, I hope that they'll choose one of our Cabernets or Merlots or Pinot Noirs. The Zinfandels we produce to be aged, oh for five to seven years, and then consumed. This is a personal style that our winery has chosen. Of course most red wines should be aged, most cork finished — the finer wines — should be aged from 10 to 20 years, hopefully. And that's not to frighten people off and say that they can't be consumed three years from the vintage date, but it's fun to know that they do improve. They're fine right now, but they get better and better. That's why people collect wine and why there are such things as wine cellars to store wine in.

• • •

Our wines are ... I like to use what's not an accurate phrase — they're "handmade." We keep machinery and handling to an absolute minimum. We pick into small fiberglass bins rather than into large gondolas, so the grapes in the bottom are not crushed and are absolutely perfect. We go through only the finest of equipment that we sent our winemaker to France to find. They only go through a crusher, a press, and in some instances they never see a centrifuge or any of these other pieces of equipment that large wineries do. We actually punch down by hand.

Our wine style from that, and our winemaker's favorite techniques, basically our own personal wine prejudices, comes out as rich, very fruity, very oaky, without losing the fruit — well-balanced in oak, we would say. A number of people feel that if you look across a range of styles, we have more oak in our wines than many. Very strong in varietal character and frequently buttery.

• • •

When winemakers talk about style they're probably talking about a wine in which there is more than one way of making them. I hear "style" most often in wines like Chardonnays and that's because there are some very distinctive styles of Chardonnays. Also I know that Gewurztraminers are coming out with drys and off-drys, and there's also some late harvest which are very sweet. So when you just see the word Gewurztraminer you don't know if you're getting very austere or very dry, but it still has the taste of the grape. You can always tell a Gewurztraminer because nothing tastes quite like that grape, but you can do different things with it.

There are a couple of distinctive styles. One of them is sometimes called the French style. And that's a Chardonnay that's light, not left in oak for a long time and has a real crisp, fresh taste to it. The other style which I happen to like myself and apparently from what I've heard is less popular now than the French style and that's the very heavy, buttery, vanilla type of Chardonnay, Chardonnay with a lot of body, left in oak with a lot of oak to it. I get a lot of flack from a couple of friends who are distributors for California wines and do a lot of promotion and PR for those wines and they accuse me of wanting to drink toothpicks, because I just want to have a lot of wood in my mouth. But I really like that style.

• • •

In some cases you deliberately make a "huge" wine you would have to lay it down for 7 years or 20 years. Sometimes you can't help it. The year does that to you. Our 1981 Chardonnay is what I call a "showy" wine, and it's got more alcohol and more oak than we normally use on our wines.

But that year, everything ripened up at once, and that's the cards we were dealt that year, so we ended up with a very nice wine, and I think people really like it, but it's a little different than what we think of our style as being. We like to have our wines be under 13 percent alcohol, and this was 13.5.

Some years you're gamblers more than others. Last year you definitely felt like you were playing poker. When the rain kept coming down, you watched your crops sitting out there ... . You can have a style, but Mother Nature or God gives you the cards that you play with that year, and you do the best you can with what you get.

• • •

You decide on a wine's style by the taste of it. Some Chardonnays have gone from some very heavy, high alcohol, intense, big wines down to fairly light, low alcohol, more finesse, maybe better food wines. Now Sauvignon Blancs — some taste very herby, very weedy, aged in oak, go through malo-lactic fermentation — and each taste may be considered a different style.

It's very simple to test it for yourself. You can go to a good wineshop and ask for different styles — make it 3 or 4 — of Sauvignon Blanc. Then drink them together side by side. Be a little hobby — very interesting.

Substandard Wine

In all commercial ventures, as in life itself, things do not always come off as planned. Wine is perhaps more vulnerable to this truism than other products, being either good, and worthy of a proud label, or substandard.

There are various ways of selling excess wines. Usually the wine's not *flawed*. It maybe seems to detract from your blend rather than add to it. So if you price it right, somebody else might want to put their label on it. Lots of little wine shops buy 400 cases of wine and put their own label on it.

Now if the wine's got a real problem, then you bulk it out and hope that somebody can blend it in with another wine where it gets lost. Or else you dump it down the drain. We've never had to do any of that, actually. We thought about doing it with our Cabernet in '78 and '79. We made both those wines kind of without benefit of winemaker, and just horsing around. What we did instead of selling it for someone else to just label it, we had so little of it we just priced it very low and sold it to one or two places. That's another way of doing it.

• • •

In some wineries you can get inconsistency even in the bottling. You'll get one case of wine that'll be great and the next case will be terrible. I see some sales on wine and I say, "How can this wine be so cheap?" and that's because there's bad bottles. Statistically you're going to get one bad bottle for so many good bottles, because there was a problem at the winery that wasn't caught, and now it's all mixed up with the good stuff. And sometimes it's all bad, and they have to dump it down the drain, the whole batch. It's your reputation.

A lot of wineries if they're not happy with the wine, they sell it in bulk. It's not under their name, and they don't let the public know they had anything to do with it. It happens all the time.

Early Wines,
Early Technology

With all due respect to the prizewinning California wines from the last century, some of which are still being sold at auction, the consensus is that there is no comparison, generally, between wines of bygone days and the wines available today. The American wine industry may even be better off technically because of the 50-year hiatus caused by Prohibition.

We have a lot of varietal wines on the market today that we did not have on the market in 1935. I guess you know that any wine named after the grape variety is a varietal wine, and the only two we had in those days were a Riesling and a Cabernet. The name of the grape used in Cabernet Sauvignon is the full name of the grape, but when I started at the winery the word Cabernet seemed to be enough, without the word Sauvignon attached to the back of it. When you said Cabernet in those days you meant Cabernet Sauvignon, so labels said simply Cabernet, because people thought putting the word Sauvignon on there was kind of redundant.

• • •

From what I've observed and from what I've heard, sure there were table wines — such as they were. The quality of table wines in this country prior to Prohibition certainly left a lot to be desired. Even some of the dessert wines had a lot of problems with the Fresno mold, known among bacteriologists as an air baccillus because of the strands in the bottom of the glasses, just like hair strands in the bottom of the bottles.

In 40 years I've seen an awful lot of changes in technology. I can remember when I first went into the wine business, iron pipes and copper pipes were common things. Now you very seldom, if ever, see them, at least in the actual handling of the wine itself. Back in those days we had a lot of steam pumps around the wineries. You don't see them any more. Stainless steel tanks were completely unknown to us. We did not have the sophisticated cooling procedures or finishing procedures we do now.

● ● ●

When I started it was about a year and a half after Prohibition ended, and we had only about a dozen wines to sell. Dessert wines were big selling items in those days. Say, prior to World War II, Ruby Port was our largest-selling wine for maybe as much as ten years. We had just a simple nucleus of a few wines of the major wine types — one Port and only one Sherry, and a Muscatel, Sauterne and Chablis, and among the reds a Claret and a Burgundy.

Our industry was trying to uplift itself, trying to raise its quality standards and all that from Repeal on to about 1950, but there were various difficulties. We worked with old vineyards. The wrong varieties of grapes were out in the field — a lot of them had to be pulled out and better grapes had to be planted. In the winery we worked with what we *had* to work with and the equipment that we had. There were old iron pumps and brass pumps and copper pipelines and things like this — these were all not very good for the wine. A lot of that had to be gotten rid of, and better equipment installed.

But stainless steel was not available to us until after World War II. It was *known* prior to World War II, but it was very expensive and there was only a little bit of it around, and people hadn't learned yet how to weld it to make something bigger like a wine tank out of a number of panels of it. The whole technology of stainless steel evolved during World War II and then again some more after that, and by 1950 had developed quite a lot.

Through these same years the University of California was studying and researching and advising the wine industry of California to plant better varieties, to find the better spots where those better varieties should be planted. The University was giving a lot of impetus to the industry in general, but also training a lot of young people who would then go out and work in the wineries. And when this young talent would come into the wine business, that had another, let's say uplifting, effect on the technology of wine to help us to produce better and better quality wines, because these people had learned very soundly, very scientifically. People like me, who had struggled along on a kind of a do-it-yourself learning process, had a great appreciation for the University of California and a great respect for the young people coming out of there.

• • •

One of the most important advances in the wine industry is probably the abundance of technologists now available. You know, at one time, back in the '50s, five of us from the same graduating class at Berkeley were producing about 80 percent of California's wines. And now they're graduating 40 and 50 a year.

In the old days the winery that had a university graduate as an enologist on the staff, you'd have to be a four- or five-thousand ton winery, one that crushed that much. Now these little new wineries that come up here, 150 tons and they've got two technologists on the staff. I don't know sometimes what they do the whole time, but there's plenty of them around, and they seem to be finding jobs.

Computers and Wine

Advanced technology is changing many facets of ordinary life, and we were curious as to how it might be affecting the wine industry. When we posed the question, however, the response was usually polite disinterest. Some of the interviewees did concede that the computer has a place in viticulture, and might play a role in the design of wine in the far, far distant future.

It would be interesting to find out what constituents cause the flavors in the wine that people like, and then to design a wine around them.

I'm not saying that you should synthetically make a wine, but modify an existing one. If there's a certain feature that people like, enhance that feature. Once you've got the basic model of what people like and what the wines consist of, and how much they like of each aspect, then by computerizing this you could design a wine that should be of optimum quality, and then strive to reach that optimum quality in wine.

There is a problem, of course. Everybody doesn't like the same thing. A lot of people will look for something different. Once you've done this, you're going to find someone else likes a different wine, and you're going to strive to make that, and pretty soon . . . . Well, variety is the spice of life . . . .

• • •

If you're talking about a very standard product that you want to computerize and year-in-year-out put out the same product, a computer might help.

The problem of trying to design wine by computer is first you've got to identify what you're going to design. We talk about a certain flavor and it means one thing to me and something else to you, and until we get together on what this flavor means and how we can identify it each time exactly the same, the computer isn't going to do you any good, because it's not going to be flexible. Once you put in a symbol for a certain flavor, or a certain concentration of a flavor in it, we'd better always be talking about exactly the same flavor.

• • •

It would make a very standardized business out of winemaking, and would apply to big firms, never to a small firm putting out premium table wines. It just wouldn't work because the blending that you do is strictly by taste, and every year you have different materials to blend with, so how do you standardize anything that changes from year to year?

• • •

Making wine by computer would be OK for people learning to drink and appreciate wine, because if the formula of sugar content and so on is the same every time the customers will know what they're getting. It would be kind of hard to do, though. When you're dealing with Mother Nature it's a different ballgame every season.

• • •

I think there's a real place for computers in the wine industry, but ours is such a personal thing. A certain amount of winemaking is an art. And I don't know if you can have a machine do something that's artful.

Our winemaker is not a lab technician. He's a winemaker. Every barrel is a little different than another barrel, and he tastes it and he smells it and he knows what's in that barrel. When I go in there weekends, and I go dabbling into a barrel, he knows exactly what barrel I've been in. It astounds me. I put the bung back in just where it was, I clean up after myself — but he *knows*. I think there are some winemakers who are technicians, and there are some winemakers who aren't and a computer would work best with a technician.

There are some real good functions for computers. We are just astounded what you can do with computers out in the vineyard, and we're very seriously thinking of getting into that — tracking down what blocks are producing this, how many bugs you found in a block, and how much water you've been putting in this one area and so on. That can really give you some long-range results that if you tried to compute with a pencil and paper you'd just give up. So there's a real function for computers.

But with a small winery, where it's such a personal thing, I just don't know . . . .

•   •   •

What a winery has to do is if they make a certain wine and they say that this year it's the same wine as they made the year before, it's got to be consistent. In other words, when somebody likes a winery's Riesling and they want to have that wine again next year, then they want it to be the same style. They want consistency.

By computer is a great idea if it works. Whatever works. I still think a person's palate is the final say-so. If the computers can do it so they can give you the taste that you want . . . But you've got to keep tasting it to be sure that the computers are doing what you want. I can see these little robots tasting the barrels . . .

It doesn't seem to go with the industry. When I visited Europe, the wineries were just so different from the wineries here. They were really old and dark and dank and there's this black mold everywhere. It's really quite charming. It reminds me of the Middle Ages. And then you'll go in a big, new winery which looks like a hospital . . . There's a lot of controversy over who makes better wine. I think you can do it both ways. The trend seems to be toward really sterile, really controlled conditions.

•   •   •

A few wineries have been using computers for years, but they don't do it to standardize the wines — they do it so they can keep track of the wines better, to make better-informed decisions about what they're going to do with each tank of wine. It's not to standardize the process, it's just so they can keep up with it better.

Let's not forget that wine is an agricultural commodity.

It is a product of the fermentation of grapes. You can't make it from chemicals. Yet. Maybe someday in the future it may be possible. I've heard rumblings about being able to take all the components of chemicals and put them together. In fact, they've tried to do that. I forget where, but I think they actually did. They took some French wine and broke it down to as many component parts as they could find and put it through all the analytical devices available to them. Then they reconstructed it, and it wasn't anything like the original. They're a long way away from being able to do anything like that.

I'm not horrified at the idea if it works. If you can produce a beverage that is the equal of a great wine and do it a whole lot cheaper, I'm all for it. I don't care how you do it, as long as it's safe to drink. I'm not one to say "Oh, we'll lose the romance of wine." *Heck!* I want the taste of wine, not the romance of it.

Through Good Times and Bad Cycles

The California wine industry has been marked by ups and downs since 1861, when Count Agoston Haraszthy collected an estimated 100,000 cuttings from European grape vines and distributed them to vintners throughout the state.

Thus the modern industry became established, to enjoy a few brief decades of prosperity, and even international fame. Then the plant louse phylloxera all but demolished the vines of wine grapes in America and Europe and much of the rest of the world.

By 1906 the wine business in Northern California had almost recuperated from this disaster, when the Earthquake destroyed millions of dollars worth of wine stored in San Francisco warehouses.

The wineries began again. Again they flourished, in part because wine was the usual complement to meals of many immigrant groups who had settled in the United States from wine-producing countries, as well as used in religious services.

Then on January 16, 1919, Amendment XVIII to the Constitution of the United States was ratified by a two-thirds vote in both houses of the Legislature. One year thereafter, the prohibition of the manufacture, sale, transport in, out of, or across the country of intoxicating beverages took effect.

Two hundred gallons of wine a year were allowed for home consumption [a very generous portion, considering that the average per capita consumption in America today hovers around the two-gallon mark]. Sacramental wine and wine prescribed for medicinal use were also legal. This was not enough, however, to keep all the wineries afloat, and many were abandoned.

If their walls could talk, many older wineries could spin a dramatic tale of that era. The Christian Brothers, whose winemaking had advanced from grapes pressed with a club in a wooden trough for their own use at table in the 1880s to a venture with current markets in all fifty states and about 60 foreign countries, acquired their Mont La Salle property in 1933.

There was a vineyard, there was already a small stone winery building, so the Brothers were delighted to buy. The previous owner had been locked up — padlocked — by the Federal Government for one or two of his employees' doing some bootlegging on this property, and so he was not allowed to make or to sell any wine — only to sell fresh grapes or fresh grape juice from the vineyard. He could not be in the wine business, so he was in tough financial shape and just had to sell.

There was a lot of bootlegging going on. It was widespread. Every hill and canyon up here had bootleggers prowling around.

• • •

Before Prohibition we had one of the largest, most successful and highly regarded wineries in California. In the 1890s . . . 1900, we used to store and age wines in San Francisco, and the 1906 earthquake destroyed the inventory. Gundlach-Bundschu Winery, Incorporated, was reestablished and on its feet again until 1918, when Prohibition came along. My grandmother, who had meanwhile bought controlling interest in the stock, was a Prohibitionist, and used her right to close the winery down. So my grandfather just went from being a grape grower-winemaker to just a grape grower. The vineyards continued, for my father and for myself, but the winery was closed all that time.

During the Depression was when we pulled out a lot of the vines and began to plant pears, because people stopped buying grapes and wine, but they did buy fresh fruit.

• • •

The Depression was a pretty good market, especially for the grape concentrate. There weren't that many wineries then either — there couldn't have been more than half a dozen, because during Prohibition many went out of business.

During the second World War, the only thing that was kind of tough was getting good help, but as far as everything else went, there was a good market for wines, because the European wines couldn't come over here. The markets back east had to be satisfied with the California wine. In fact, I think the second World War helped us get our label recognized and established around the country simply because there was a shortage of wine.

• • •

In the '40s and '50s very few people were drinking wine. It was a very difficult way to make a living.

Boom

It is difficult to pinpoint exactly why or when, but in what appeared to be a very short span of time the renaissance of the Northern California wine industry turned into an outright boom.

Ten years ago there were seven of us in the Sonoma Valley Grape Growers Association, and today there are 17 of us, just in Sonoma Valley. I think there are 120 wineries in Sonoma County now.

• • •

Napa County has attracted more new wineries than any other area of the state, and has the largest number of wineries of any other county of the whole state. Napa County is a relatively small county — much smaller than Sonoma County and many other counties in California, but still it has the greatest number of wineries. This means we were doing things right and we attracted attention, and so we have little wineries of all kinds that have sprung up in the past 10 or 15 years — I've sometimes said they're springing up like mushrooms under every oak tree.

There are more than 135 wineries in Napa County now. Right after Prohibition ended there were only about eight or so that were active. I take this big explosion in numbers to be a great credit to all those people who were here first.

• • •

I think it's the wine technology a little bit after World War II and 1950 that has caused the big shift. The fact that we made really fine wines and people could see and taste and be impressed by the quality of those wines — their good palatability, their reliability, and their general continuity of quality from year to year — then they would be inspired to get into the same business in the same area.

You know, when you're looking back over history, you don't want to take just a lot of isolated things and think they're unrelated. Most things were related to other things happening about the same time.

• • •

Things like this don't happen in *a* year or *a* day. From the moment Prohibition was repealed in '33 people have been working to promote wine and let Americans discover wine. The Wine Institute was formed in 1934 and the Wine Advisory Board shortly thereafter, and most of the wineries would belong to it and pay certain fees. Remember, when Prohibition was repealed, every state had the right to control alcoholic beverages, and therefore gradually over a period of time each state had to be worked on to make wine acceptable, so we would try to influence legislation as much as we could by legal means, and we would put on wine tastings and industry-type tastings, not brand-type tastings.

It *seems* suddenly the efforts came to fruition — like when you go to pick a peach. The peach doesn't show up in one day, it's been a whole year in the making. And the same thing with wine. We were working since Repeal, and it grew, grew, grew, and finally it got to the proportions where it appeared to be a boom.

• • •

It wasn't *a* specific year. It was 1970 through 1972 when there was just a small nucleus of wineries — Freemark

Abbey, Martini, Inglenook, Joe Heitz ... Sebastiani was just getting into it and Sellards and Joe Swan in Sonoma — that stopped to look, and there were not many grapes planted. There were less than 200 acres of Merlot. That's a thousand cases of Merlot available in the entire United States.

All of a sudden these wineries were selling all of the wines that they had, because of the affluence of the early '70s. Growers then saw what the prices were for grapes, and began to plant more grapes. Wineries saw what these few wineries were doing, and other people interested in the business began to build more wineries. As wineries proliferated, more growers planted grapes, and it built on itself, and of course the key is that people are drinking more wine.

The boom was generated from without because people had money, and was generated from within because it produced a new generation of wine writers, winery owners, vineyard investors who were doctors and lawyers. Once you sink your money into something you're going to support it and drink it. So it was generated on two fronts, one from within and one from the consumers.

• • •

Americans are not consuming much more than two gallons a year, that's true, but that's a lot more than one gallon a year, and it used to be one gallon. Back in the '60s or someplace it was a little bit over one gallon. I think this increase is just natural. First of all, we were far enough away from Prohibition. People travelling in Europe ... Just by word of mouth it got around. There are still some parts of the country that are very sterile as far as wine consumption goes, but mostly in your metropolitan cities it's gotten up to a pretty good standard.

• • •

Travelling definitely has caused people to drink more wine. Also, a few people carried it on — probably the ones who were more affluent and travelled, the small nucleus of people who continued to drink wine — Andre Tchelistcheff and some of the wineries that went through Prohibition — and appreciated it and introduced it to others.

• • •

The boom in wine drinking brought on the boom in new vineyards and vintners. It would never have started if they didn't think they were going to have a successful enterprise. Right now, I think we have an oversupply of grapes, but that's a cyclic type of thing and in a few years it'll be getting around and we'll have a shortage again.

• • •

People are consuming more wine, but there's more wine to consume.

Parlous Times

The benign and beautiful Napa and Sonoma Valleys mark the entrance to California's wine country north of San Francisco. Long before the present boom in wine consumption and in wineries, the Sonoma Valley was a historical mecca because of the still visible legacies of the Franciscan fathers and of Agoston Haraszthy. The Napa Valley has its own history as a pleasant summer retreat for affluent Northern California families.

Within the area are three of the zones defined by U.C. Davis as containing optimum soil content, elevation, mean temperature, and climate for the growing of Chardonnay, Cabernet Sauvignon, Zinfandel, Pinot Noir, Sauvignon Blanc, Johannisberg Riesling, Gewurztraminer, and Merlot grapes; other varieties thrive there as well. Both valleys might be left for all time to vineyards alone, but pleasing vistas, salubrious climate, and the fact that the financial and industrial centers of Northern California are within a short commute make them a magnet for an expanding population with other ideas.

The Sonoma Valley sprawls near one of the largest, most travelled throughfares in California — Highway 101 — and new housing developments are becoming noticeable among the vineyards. The Napa Valley would seem to be a natural enclave, lacking only a drawbridge to protect those already inside.

As the northbound tourist often notes with frustration, Napa Valley Highway 29 suddenly narrows from a six lane blacktop to a maddening single lane in either direction. Currently, according to a state law that is heartily endorsed by local vintners, the freeway cannot come any farther north than it does, thus dampening all but the most ardent desire to commute on a daily basis. Also, some protection against encroachment is afforded by the Williamson Act, which gives a tax break to agriculturalists.

According to a real estate broker who specializes in vineyard property, in late 1983 the going rate for a one-acre building site in Napa Valley, if one were available (which it was not), would be 60 thousand dollars.

"Assuming 20 acres of vineyard land at 20 thousand dollars an acre and a fully-equipped small winery of 10,000 square feet, you're talking one million three-hundred thousand dollars before you squeeze the first grape, and the vines take five years to begin producing.

"The same thing happened in the San Joaquin. People pulled up prunes, plums, orchards ... When they didn't make it, the big corporations moved in."

As of this writing, none of the picturesque old wineries abandoned during Prohibition are on the market, having been refurbished into new wineries or remodeled into chic living quarters.

But these are parlous times in the wine industry. A combination of factors, including overproduction of grapes, new technology, competition from subsidized foreign wines, and currency devaluation, has resulted in a current surplus of wine. Despite ruinous torrential rains near harvesttime in 1983, which may halt the wine glut situation within a few years, the present owners of several new wineries in both valleys want out of the business, and Multiple Listing is heavy with winery real estate for sale.

The recent asking price of one brand new winery with all

accoutrements and surrounded by seven acres of young vines was 800 thousand dollars.

"But if the owner gets desperate, someone could walk in and get it for half a million in a distress sale," said the broker.

"Of course, if you need a substantial tax write-off, a winery would be one way to do it."

There were quite a few wineries in this Valley prior to Prohibition, and of course a lot of them went by the wayside. That's why you hear about people finding these historic, abandoned spots. When I came here almost 15 years ago there were about 40 wineries. There are about 140 today, and you got bankers, lawyers, Indian chiefs, you name it, making wine. Some of them may fall by the wayside because they're under-financed or because they're using it for a tax dodge or just don't have the ability to do what they're trying to do.

The fact remains that consumption of wine has gone up very, very slowly, and when you talk about increases in wine consumption, you're talking of tenths of percents. We've been talking about one-and-a-half and two-point-two gallons per capita for the last ten or 12 years.

Ten years ago, a financial institution in the state of California came out and indicated that we are going to be out of wine because people are going to drink it up so fast. Maybe that was an encouragement for people to come and make loans to get into the wine business. I don't know.

People were not taking into consideration the fact that we are not a wine-drinking country. Maybe in a hundred years I'm going to come back and check into this business and see what people are drinking. Right now, if we were running out of wine . . .

In 1982 we had probably the largest grape crop in the history of the state of California — around five million two thousand tons. There are probably millions of gallons of wine floating around the state that people don't know what the hell to do with. A lot of it may be burned up.

Maybe it went into alcohol, maybe into brandy, but there's a limitation there too.

We have a long way to go in total increase in wine consumption. To hear those experts, you would have thought that wine consumption by 1984 was probably going to be around three or four gallons. I wish it were. We'd have a lot of our problems solved.

• • •

The vineyards are going to be there, but the names are going to be different. I think a lot of people come up here thinking they like the lifestyle, they like the area, they're looking for a way of making a living away from the city and the commute and all that. But I think if that's you're only reason for being up here, you may be one of the people that are going to drop off to the side as this business becomes more and more competitive. It really is competitive right now, and so you have to have a better reason for doing it than that. In other words, there's going to be some people selling their wineries, because they just can't keep up with the track. In most cases the wineries will continue to function as such under somebody else who'll buy the building and change the name.

• • •

There are some famous people who made money in other walks of life and then got into the wine business because it is quote "a glamorous way of making a living," but now people are finding out it's just a lot of hard work like any other business. It's just not quite so stressful. And then there are those who are just farmers who, I guess you would call it, vertically-integrated into growing grapes in small lots of estate-bottled wines. So there are two different avenues — 90 percent of the people are totally dedicated to the wine business, and probably 10 percent got into it misguided, under false beliefs in what the wine business is, and those are the people who probably won't be in the business ten years from now.

• • •

A lot of these so-called newcomers — these broker

types, bankers, what have you — are doing a fine job. Others have planted on marginal land where grapes should never have been planted in the first place, and as long as we are in an artificially high market, they'll make a living. But when things return to normal, some of those on marginal territory or with marginal knowledge are going to have to disappear.

● ● ●

There are a number of new big wineries and the rest are estate. The new ones are big because they're backed by big corporations. Heublein owns the Napa Valley.

● ● ●

This is not the first glut in history. If there's a real surplus, you can distill excess grapes into high-proof brandy. And then that can be sold to chemical companies as a solvent, or different things. Now there's a lot of talk about mixing alcohol with gas for motor fuel, but it's more expensive than gasoline, so that's not a very good way to get rid of it. Then there's the basic thing. Vineyards that don't make money are pulled. Pull out the vines and plant cucumbers or walnuts or something. It has happened in the past. I would hope it would not, but it'll happen in California.

● ● ●

There's a category of people who just . . . I think it's the romanticism. They want to have a winery, and they don't think too much about the quality or the marketing. There are a number of them. It's unfortunate. If you find a very small winery selling their wine at Safeway, I think they're in trouble, because from what we see of our own balance sheet, were we not in a premium-quality league, we could not survive. If you can't charge the prices we charge for our wines, we couldn't possibly survive. We make the barest of profit margins as it is — and it is more expensive to make premium-quality wine. There are some basic costs that everybody has, and a very small winery just making mediocre wine and selling it for mediocre prices — I don't know how they can survive except hand to mouth. And not even that in many cases, with the competition the way it is.

• • •

In California as a whole there is an oversupply of grapes, and the extra grapes go into brandy and some concentrate production. They're trying to find some other uses for these grapes, like jellies and stuff like that, but that's a very small amount. Basically, I think it's being used up somewhere. As far as I know, none of it's being thrown away. And there's some wine exports, too, starting to take hold, and a few exports of grapes. Some grapes are going for home wine production — lots of people make wines at home. They seem to be finding a home, but not at the prices that the growers would like to have.

Wine and the Government

Regulations

In effect, the American wine industry dates only from 1935, one year after the ratification of Amendment 21. When Repeal came it was like beginning again.

At the same time, a prohibition of another kind — "the transportation or importation into any State, Territory, or possession of the United States for delivery or use therein of intoxicating liquors in violation of the laws thereof" — was written into the U.S. Constitution. To conform, each state passed its own restrictions, and to this day the wine-producing states must adhere to as many regulations in importation and exportation of wine across state lines as there are states of the Union.

In addition, regulations and tariffs, sometimes prohibitive, must be considered in the exportation of wine to foreign countries, most of which do not face such protectionism when they send their wines here. Furthermore, those wines often have government subsidies and can be sold in America at well under local prices. Even Canada, for example, has strong government regulation on imports to protect their own small wine industry.

The Wine Institute — the trade association which among other things represents the interests of the California wine industry with both federal and state governments — also works to make international restrictions equal and mutual. Wine Institute spokesmen maintain that if wine were to be considered by each state as the agricultural product it is, to be bought in groceries as food and not as "booze", it would go a long way to cutting out some of the regulations which hamper the flow, so to speak, of wine back and forth across the nation.

The government regulations are certainly restrictive in our business, and a lot of times they're not rational ... even downright ridiculous! It's a big drain. But we don't fight them. We just live with them the best we can.

• • •

Something that would really help the California wine industry would be for the states to have a general way of allowing you to import wine into them. As it is now, it's almost like dealing with 49 other countries, because each state has its own rules and regulations, and some states are virtually impossible for a small producer to bring their wines into because the tariffs are so high. The wine industry would be really in a boom period if there was some way that there was just a federal control over all of the states, and each state didn't have its own legislation for wines.

• • •

Let me tell you how small we are. We're small enough that we tell the out-of-staters if they want our wine, we don't give a discount and they have to pay the freight. And they have to get the forms and pay the licensing fees. That's a luxury we're going to probably have to give up down the road. At this point, they're anxious enough for wine, they'll do this for us. But the regulations are nightmarish. There are some states that we wonder why we even sell to. Well, the reason is, someone else is doing the paper work. They send us forms to sign and that's it.

• • •

There's a different set of regulations for each state that you have to know. And not only do you have to know what they are, but then you have to know what the *realities* are because the people within the state frequently have found a way of getting around the regulations. So you have to know what the *real* system is.

• • •

I don't think the people in Washington D.C. know how to make wine as well as I do, but that's not the way the world works. I must admit some of these things seem stupid and unnecessary to me. But as I've gotten older and travelled around the nation and seen some of the things people are doing under existing regulations, I can understand why government regulation is necessary. There are always those who are going to cheapen or bastardize their product at the short-term gain for a few bucks for themselves and the long-range hurt of the industry. I gripe about the regulations, but I think they're probably needed.

Appellations of Origin

The Napa and Sonoma Valleys do not just meander vaguely among the Mayacmas, Sonoma, and Vaca Mountains of the Northern California Coast Range. They are officially designated Viticultural Areas registered by the U.S. Department of the Treasury's Bureau of Alcohol, Tobacco & Firearms [BATF] in Washington, D.C., with boundaries set according to features on a U.S. Geological Survey map.

These Viticultural Areas went into effect, after lengthy and often controversial hearings, on January first, 1983. As of that date, wine labeled as originating in Napa Valley or Sonoma Valley must derive at least 85 percent from grapes grown physically within the officially defined borders.

The characteristics of different grape varieties are shaped by climate, soil type, elevation, and finite physical features, such as which way irrigation water flows, and on this basis Appellation is derived.

The American version of Appellation of Origin came about possibly in response to the consumer information movement of the '60s and '70s, and was not initiated to determine the price of grapes. However, somehow it often does.

The way the BATF has drawn things, Napa and Napa Valley pretty much conforms to at least the lower part of the County's boundaries. The BATF had outlined everything that you had to present to them to get your appellations defined and approved, and it was soil, climate, history, and a number of other things, but basically you had to make a case for why this particular area you suggested with your boundaries is the one that should be approved. We spent endless days of testimony in Sonoma Valley, and Napa apparently spent at least that long. And they had very carefully divided, drawn their lines as to what they thought the appellation ought to be. In the end the BATF just must have ignored all the soil, climate, historical background, because what they approved was the boundary on political lines, which of course were not drawn with the soil, climate, historical etcetera in mind. Not a good way to delineate a wine-growing region. To have said at the beginning now we're going to make this decision on the basis of soil, climate — now obviously that's not what they did.

• • •

Things like restrictions about the appellation and the percentages of the varietal that have to be in the bottle now, force the wineries to make certain business decisions, what kind of grapes to buy, and so on. To the people who go by appellations, it's very critical who's in the appellation, and who's out. It was a very long and tedious process deciding what is the Napa Valley. One of the basic considerations was well, Carneros is one region, but also one of the valleys sort of over the hill over there is in Napa *County*, but hardly in Napa Valley. Well, they fought long and hard, and it seems they are included in the appellation. But there's other little valleys, other little areas . . . .

You know, 100 acres of grapes in those little areas and you weren't included in Napa Valley, you could very well go bankrupt. It's as simple as that. Because the price you get for your grapes for certain varieties can go from 800 dollars a ton to 400 dollars a ton.

• • •

The wines don't get a higher price, but the grapes certainly do. When our accountant saw what we were getting paid for our Merlot that we sell to another winery, he was aghast. But as far as I know that's the best price that anybody gets for that varietal in Sonoma County. A couple of hundred dollars less per ton than Napa.

• • •

I think the appellation was done basically for commercial reasons which are yet to be realized. Now that we've got it, I wish we were doing more with local government, etc., to promote the appellation. The appellation at this time isn't terribly important. We want to promote the appellations, but we don't want to do it in a way that adds additional confusion to the consumer, who is already thoroughly confused by all the numbers of wineries on the market today. It's such a rapid increase, nobody can keep them straight.

• • •

There are now four wineries in Bennett Valley. The Sonoma Valley Vintners Association wrote up an appellation proposal for the Sonoma Valley and we were included in it. It sailed right through. Otherwise Bennett Valley would have been in no man's land. We have the same climate and the same soil type, and we're just over the hill. It's a logical inclusion. It's very valuable to us.

• • •

As a winemaker, appellation doesn't affect me at all. I have California wines, and I have Napa Valley wines. If you read the label you can see that. It's very obvious. The Number 2 line on the bottle, I think. The wines that we grow and crush here are Napa Valley wines and so state on the label. Now, for some of our other wines, we buy them — wines like the Port and the Sherry and some of our lesser wines, like Chablis. We buy these and blend them and age them and bottle them, and if they come from outside the Valley we put California on it. We always have, so I don't think the Napa Valley appellation affects me one way or the other.

• • •

The more sophisticated the consumer becomes, the less appellation of origin will matter. Over the past few years there has been an awareness that certain vineyard designations are an assurance of high quality. Just as the more sophisticated French wine buyers know that Chateau Lafite wine is excellent, they also become aware that in some years lesser-known growths will rival the grapes produced at Chateau Lafite.

Given the current state of the market, wineries are beginning not only to put the appellation of origin on the label, which they must do by government decree, but are opting also to put the vineyard name on the label in an old California tradition that pinpoints the actual source of the grape. The designation gets more finite as it goes from the district, the political (county) area, to the Napa Valley, for instance, right on down to the vineyard. Field Number 42-XYZ is not as glamorous-sounding as, for example, Martha's Vineyard, but that could always be fixed with a little imagination.

●   ●   ●

Appellations. That's a tough issue. It's right to put appellations on the label, but I think it's too early to say what that means. It's going to take a few years — probably the rest of my lifetime at least, and maybe more than that — to sort it all out. But it's important to start putting the appellations on there now so that we *can* sort it all out. The only thing I would warn the consumer about is don't buy on appellation. The most important piece of information on that label is who made the wine. Who's name is on top of that label?

The Commerce of Wine
Pricing Wine

A definition of premium wine proved elusive, as well as controversial. The only consensus among vintners seemed to be that Premium Wine is definitely not jug wine.

Several years ago, when prices were a lot more modest than they are now, there was a premium wine group formed in Southern California. It was really sales reps from various wineries and they'd have a meeting I think once a month, and their definition of premium was "Any wine that sells for over X dollars a bottle." I think it was three dollars in those days. But that doesn't mean premium to me. I've spent 20 dollars for a bottle of wine and had it be junk. And I've had some very good jug wines for three or four dollars.

What's premium to you, isn't to me. It's what you like and what I like. What do you consider a fine pair of shoes? It's different things for different people.

• • •

Last year an economist wrote that the greatest growth in the wine industry was in the seven- to twelve-dollar class. People think they're getting a better wine. They *are* getting a lot better wine than a good many years ago and I think prices have an awful lot to do with it. We have priced our wines in a very modest fashion, and we have 100 percent Chardonnay in our Chardonnays, for example, and 100 percent Cabernet, and we do not try to gouge the consuming public, but we make a fair profit.

Go into your big chain store and look at your prices on the so-called jug wines — the magnums, three-liter or four-liter jugs. The wines going in there are made from the less expensive grapes, primarily from the San Joaquin Valley. Regardless of who makes them, that's where all the jug wines come from, and you can see terrific cut rates on all that stuff.

What it all adds up to, if you can keep your head above

water in this premium business and put good quality in the bottle at a competitive price that doesn't make the individual drinking the wine choke on every swallow, then I think that is the long-term program we should have.

The American premium wine business has never been more than five or ten percent of the total wine business. Secondly, the American premium business, particularly the California premium wine business, is not based, nor will it ever be based, on occasional sales of 45 or 50 dollars a bottle, which sometimes is palmed off on the public as being something super-duper. As one of our distributors back in Washington recently told me, "If I had to depend on the one or two bottles of that wine that I sell a month, I'd be out of business."

People are very price-conscious, but they want quality. Unfortunately, in this I'm including people who say, "Gee, this has to be good if it's 20 dollars, but this must be a helluva lot better because it's 40." That certainly is not true in the wine business. I think there is little or no correlation between price and quality today in the market.

I think a lot of people take advantage of comments that somebody has made or written about their wines and built themselves up such an ego that they say, "Well, if theirs is 20 we'd better put 30 bucks on our bottle because I think we can get it."

• • •

In the long run, price has to have something to do with the goodness of wine. If I have a product of premium quality, and if I sell it too cheap, I'm not going to have enough income to pay for making a wine that good, and I'm going to go broke. On the other hand, if I charge more than it's worth, people are going to wise up, because they're not stupid. And they won't buy it and I'll go broke because I don't have any income. We taste very seriously and I know other people do, too, to get their product priced in the proper range for what it's worth.

When we release a new vintage, we will have blind tastings, and we'll taste it against past vintages and we know what they sold for and how well they sold, and we'll taste it against what other wines are on the market just about in the range that we believe ours to be in, both foreign and California — obviously, just buy those right now so we know what those are selling for — and we'll see where ours fits in. Depending on where it places in our tasting, we'll price it at the top of the list or in the middle, or at the bottom of what the world is doing. If you lock yourself in your own closet all the time, you're not going to be very bright when you come out after awhile. You have to keep your head out of the sand.

• • •

I think the price tells you maybe what the demand for the wine is, rather than maybe how good that wine is. We're seeing a reaction which I'm just loving. It's difficult right now to be selling wine in our category, but I like it because it used to be when we took our wines into a store, they'd say "This is really nice wine but you didn't price it high enough. If you'd only priced it at 18 dollars a bottle we could sell *cases* of the stuff." Or trying to get into a restaurant and having them say "We don't buy wines that are priced at your level." You know, we're not cheap, but they wanted the super-high-priced wines. And the consumer was equating excellence with a high pricetag. I think now with the way the economy is, maybe the consumer is getting more knowledgeable, and looking for a good value in wine. I don't think they're equating price and quality like they used to, which I think is just wonderful.

Retailing Wine

Recent economic upheaval has affected the way that wine is sold in retail stores. Discount stores everywhere seem to be gaining popularity with the consumer over traditional wine outlets, and the issue is fraught with strong opinion and controversy.

It would be a lot harder to do what I did *this* year than when we got started. Five years ago small wineries were still met with some real interest, whereas now people are just overcome with small wineries and the number of labels, and they're saying "Hey, I don't have *space* for any more labels in my shop." Then, even though there were a lot of small wineries, people were still interested in hearing your story.

In the past you would expect to get orders for 20 or 30 cases at a crack. The philosophy of a wineshop used to be "There are very limited quantities of wine from XYZ Winery and they're presenting it to us, and if we want it, we'd better order big now, because we won't have a second chance to order it." Well, that's not the case any more. Most wineries do not sell out the first day they release the wine like we did for several years. Now it's, "I know you'll still have wine, so why should I tie up so much of my money for all this wine all at once, unless you give me some incentives or breaks for buying it in quantity. I'll buy my five cases and we'll see in a month if you still have any around. You know, 15 or 20 other wineries are making some pretty exciting wines, and we'll catch on with them."

It's a whole different philosophy than it used to be in the marketplace.

• • •

Retailers now are very conservative with their buying since the advent of Liquor Barn.

• • •

I was just at a wine marketing seminar given by Sonoma State. The wine business right now is in a real period of transition. The discount houses are very much coming onto the scene and it's questionable how the boutique wine shops will fare during this period, because the small wineries are not used to price competition. It's *never* been the case, and now all of a sudden they are faced with price competition because of the proliferation of new labels and new wineries and lots of product.

• • •

Liquor Barn has a large number of stores and they carry just about any wine you'd want to find. The bottle price is what a wine shop would give you only on a case — ten or fifteen percent off. They're very aggressive in their marketing and they take full pages of ads in the newspaper. People are shopping there, and I would too. You find a lot of wines there, and you find good prices.

It's just been in the last couple of years that Liquor Barn has been a force in the marketplace. We resisted selling to Liquor Barn. We kind of sat back and watched for a little while to see what was going on because we felt a certain commitment to the wine shops that had helped build our name — not that we're a household word by any means. People bought our wine because the wine shops we dealt with recommended our wines, and we certainly didn't want to turn right around and sell to the discount down the street.

It's amazing that Liquor Barn has had such an impact on the wine shops, because there's been a lot of other discount stores. In Southern California, there's Trader Joe's that's been around for a number of years, but it has never seemed to scare the retailer like Liquor Barn has. Maybe it's just timing. The economy being the way it is, maybe people are looking for deals more than they did in the past. The retailer is going through a period of self-evaluation, where they have to decide how they're going to cope. What's going to make them stand out?

• • •

People who go to Liquor Barn know what they're looking for. They know about the wines, the vineyards, and the years, because they got their knowledge about wines in shops like ours. We can still match their prices in volume buys — by the case — but sheer economics is making stores like ours a luxury item.

• • •

A lot of wineries are *not* there on the shelves of Liquor Barn, but I'm sure we would see wines we didn't know existed. It's part of the shake-up in the wine business. They're going to put a lot of retailers out of business. They're going to suddenly change the face of the wine retail business. It's got to have a tremendous effect.

The good is that they're introducing people to wines who may never have seen wines. I've seen some of the promotional things put out by Safeway, which owns Liquor Barn. It's very simple education for the person who doesn't ordinarily consume wine and is only confused by labels and doesn't know the difference between Chablis and a Chardonnay. They're doing some very basic education that I applaud, because it's just going to open more doors to people to find fine wine.

The bad part is the people who are doing the most educating and who are at the heart of getting wine from producer to public are traditional wine shops and liquor stores that have gotten into premium wines. They do a tremendous educational job for the wine business. And they're the ones who are going to be in trouble, because they can't run a fine shop and do it at the prices that Liquor Barn can do it.

If I put myself into the place of a consumer, I would rather walk into a small shop where you can talk to somebody who knows in detail about all these wines rather than a discount store, which must be an overpowering experience when you walk in. Just as I'd rather walk into a small shop where a salesperson says "Here and here and here is what you're looking for." Plus we feel that small business contributes to the health of the economy. As businesses get larger and larger and larger, the small ones have to fade. It's not a healthy direction at all. All we can do is continue to be a small business ourselves and favor small retailers that are strong in the superfine and the super premium wines.

Promoting Wine

Because of its beauty and romantic aura, the wine country of Northern California is now second only to Disneyland in the number of tourists it attracts. Italian Swiss Colony, now a part of Allied Vintners, was a pioneer in wine marketing with pizzazz. Their elaborately corny chalet may not have been the first or only tasting room in the area at that time, but it was certainly the most entertaining as a goal for outings. They sold a lot of wine that way.
Until very recently, the Winery Tasting Room was about it, as far as "marketing" went.

Marketing in wines when I went into the business was practically non-existent. I mean, what did we have? We had whiskeys. We had brandies. We had Port, Muscatel and Sherries, Tonic Ports and the dry wines — that was a sideline. And what was the image in the paper? The only time you ever heard anything about Port or Muscatel was when somebody wrote an article about a guy on skid row that they found an empty bottle beside.

I think we suddenly became — particularly in the last 20 years — aware of the fact that we should go out and educate people, and today I think it's more important than ever.

If you want to be polite, you say the premium wine business is highly competitive. I almost said a highly competitive rat-race — that's just about what it is. It's a real jungle out there.

More and more people today are becoming interested in wine, but the fact remains that as far as wine consumption goes, the figure is basically static. Probably 85 percent of the wine is drunk by 15 percent of the population. Basically, we are not a wine-drinking country.

The tasting of wine is a very subjective thing, and you've got a sophisticated consumer out there. You don't tell him to drink what you made because you think it's the greatest. He's going to tell you what he likes. He or she has been exposed to a lot of wines, and is investigating them, and that's where our real wine market is.

• • •

There's so much competition, even amongst the very small wineries, that you have to keep yourself in the public eye, so we do a lot of work to stay there. We're in a funny position because we're so small that people don't want to do very much publicity for us. We're not the size winery that a writer feels comfortable writing a nationwide article about because they're always concerned that whoever reads the article won't be able to go out and easily find wines they've just read about. I think we really end up having to do more. For one thing, we're the staff. There's us, a winemaker, an assistant winemaker, a secretary, and that's it. We wear so many different hats. Somehow it feels like more work if you're the only one out there.

• • •

Wine to drink every day at home is definitely not far in the future, but the wine industry has found over the last ten years that the same people are drinking more and more wine. However, in many areas there are still people who do not consume wine in any consistent manner with food every night. They'll do it as a cocktail, an aperitif, maybe on Saturday night, but they don't appreciate entirely the way wine and food go together. After all, look at the beer industry — it grows much faster than the wine industry. And yet, I can't envision a meal without wine, and probably you can't either, but there are a tremendous number of people out in the country that still have to learn about wines.

Wine has always been somewhat intimidating, and we have to be very careful to present it as a beverage which is enjoyable and which is certainly not a high alcoholic beverage. It's an entertaining beverage in itself, not like opening a can of beer or drinking a glass of milk, which is fine, but not many adults drink milk.

But it's certainly a challenge. We do not want to confuse people with the bouquet, and the aroma, and the nose, and the texture and the viscosity and the legs. We just want people to enjoy a glass of wine just for the taste, and once they get started on that, it's such an interesting, plus satisfying beverage, they will build themselves on that. But if we frighten them off by pretending that they have to know all of these things about wine, that's ridiculous, because all you have to do is like the wine that's in the glass and drink it and enjoy it, and eliminate all of the snob appeal that goes with it. That can come later on, according to one's personal bent.

• • •

We've just opened up the Chicago market. We have a distributor there who is very enthusiastic, and he's putting on a large tasting for people from wine societies, people from restaurants and retail shops. They're asking their wineries to come out and so we can face-to-face with the people actually buying our wine. It's going to be a two-day affair. All our relationships with the distributor have been on the phone, so it's very important for us to go back there and see what they're doing and give them support with the sales effort.

In the past the ways of doing sales for small wineries was very simple because you didn't have to do any travelling. People were very excited to have any boutique winery. The quality almost didn't matter. Now there are so many small wineries and the French wines are now a value again because the franc has been devalued and so on, so people who never travelled before are hitting the trail and going out and promoting their wines, even though it might mean that they're only selling 300 cases of wine in the state. You have to do it.

• • •

The wine industry is becoming more specialized and some marketing people have a clearer insight than specialized people. There's different expertise for everything, distributing and so on, and it's very important in the industry that the people *are* experts in whatever facet of marketing they're dealing with, because it's just too complex and too competitive to be a "novice" anything!

• • •

I'm just a farmer, and I make wine. I've given the marketing to a professional marketing firm in New York. Marketing is far removed from growing grapes and making wine. It's a totally different avenue — a different business. I feel I can best put my time to use making wine and growing grapes and leave the marketing to them. Of course, we're in constant communication about what wines we'll be producing and what styles of wine people find the most appealing.

• • •

We've gotten some outstanding press. According to our size we probably do pretty well. One thing in PR and marketing that is becoming clear is that you've got to always be representing your winery. You have got to have an appearance. You've got to visit retailers, put yourself in the public eye.

We always go to the tastings we do as a group — the Vintners Association, the Wine Growers Association. It's very important that the public has some sense that the people actually making the wine are real people actually standing behind that table pouring the wine. Most of the other wineries send staff — meaning down a very long chain of command — to pour wine, or it may be a distributor's person who maybe doesn't know anybody at the winery or has been on a tour a couple of times. And people at a tasting will start asking questions about "Do *they* do such and such a thing?" And when they find out it's not "they", it's us, they're so excited and honored, almost, that the people involved in the winery are actually pouring the wine for them and talking to them about it, that I think in these cases we steal the show because of that, and because of the quality of our wine.

I don't think there are many wineries that can afford not to be PR or marketing-oriented or conscious. That's all there is to it. It's a lesson that you learn as you get into the business.

With a lot of people that get into it, marketing and public relations come first. *Then* you think about providing the product to fit into your marketing scheme. We did exactly the opposite. We've got the product, we're product-oriented. We didn't know anything about marketing and public relations when we started. We had to learn that. A lot of people come into the business and they know business. They know marketing. They know that part of it, so it's natural to be able to go out and get involved in sales. We all have to do it. Our accountant laughs at us — a classic example of a product-oriented business. You know, "Mom makes great chili — why don't we set up a chili stand?" And then when they do, they discover it costs so much to make chili they can't make a profit on the business. We've come at it from that direction, whereas a great number of wineries have come at it from the opposite direction — all the business sense, all the marketing — and the wine is almost an afterthought.

● ● ●

We're very small, only 10,000 cases, so the PR we're doing is what we do ourselves, and sometimes I think it suffers because of that. On the other hand, you have to take one step at a time and we've just recently got into 10,000 cases so at this point we have to do everything ourselves.

Everything we've done, we've started from scratch and done ourselves. It gives us a better perspective of what our needs are. We evaluate ourselves. When we see we're weak in an area, then we hire someone to carry on. And we can have a better appreciation of what they need to do, rather than if we just decided we need someone for PR and we hire somebody and they go off and spend a lot of money and we don't really understand what they're doing or why they're doing it. So our approach has been to be very conservative in spending our money, but rather spend a lot of effort and our own time.

In the beginning we did all of our sales ourselves, all of our deliveries ourselves, we did *everything* — every case of wine that was sold there was an interface between either us and the exact salesperson or at least with the owner of the store. Now we're getting a little bigger, we have a service that does the delivering for us, and we also have some brokers who are out in the street for us. But we have an understanding of what we need for them to do, because we've done it. That's been our approach.

I have no background in sales. My brother said, "Hey, we've got some jobs here for the winery and I'm going to be the manager, so you can't do that. We're going to hire a winemaker so you can't do that. The only thing left is sales. What do you think?" And I laughed and said "Don't you remember all the Girl Scout cookies we got stuck with because I wouldn't go door to door?" And he said, "Well, think about it." I just went out and I did it like I would be researching a paper. I went out and talked to everyone I could talk to who did well on sales, marketing wines, and then I talked to the people who bought the wine, and said, "If I'm approaching you in a few months with a bottle of wine to sell, how do you wish small wineries would approach you?" So when I did have a product, people knew me already, and it wasn't half as hard as if I'd gone out cold.

Also I was very lucky, because that first wine that I marketed won a Gold Medal at the Los Angeles County Fair. I didn't know it at the time I was marketing it, but it was a *good* wine, so people were very receptive to it. There were only 200 cases of it, so this was not a grandiose marketing project by any stretch of the imagination, but I was able to call people and say, "Do you realize we've just won a gold medal?" And at that point I had sold 190 cases out of the 200. So people were calling us and saying "I want the wine. Where can we get it?" It was fun.

• • •

In the past, a small winery would probably sell 90 percent of their production in California. Those days are past. You're having to spread it out, and stretch outside of California. Northern California is an exceptionally good wine market, but it's a much tougher market. It was tough even five years ago, because that's the first place everybody takes their wine. Southern California strikes me as being a bit more trendy. They want what's new, and it's easy to sell them almost anything the first year. What's new is really important.

• • •

We're spoiled, growing up in the Bay Area. Even if you were interested in wine back in the '60s you had Freemark Abbey and Martini and Beaulieu and Joe Heitz and some of the finest wines then available which weren't even being exported out of Northern California to any large degree. So it doesn't take you much travelling around the country to realize that people are just beginning to learn about fine wines and fine cuisine. It's centered on the Coasts, and we are spoiled, particularly in Northern California, growing up with fine restaurants and so close to the fine wineries, so we tend to take this for granted, whereas it takes almost a pioneer to establish a restaurant with a fine wine list in some other places. It takes a pioneer spirit, and those are the type of people to work very closely with, because they are educating the consumers. They have the knowledge. That's not to say that consumers are not sophisticated, it's just that we've been exposed to so much more, particularly in Northern California.

• • •

Sure we do public relations, but we don't have a "department" for anything. This is a family winery, there are five family members and five other people that work for us and we do everything — mow the yard, cut firewood on through crushing grapes through wine processing through the bottling and the merchandising. Like today we're having the fellow who distributes our wine in the Washington D.C. and Maryland area here for lunch. He's a friend of ours. We have people for lunch all the time. That's public relations. But we don't have a department. We try to let other people know we exist, yes. We promote wine by word of mouth. Most people in public relations departments think you have to give people a snow job and that the better mousetrap theory is a bunch of hokum. I don't believe that. I think the better mousetrap theory works. It's worked for us. We make good wines and people come to us.

• • •

We figured we'd have to do some marketing because of the influx of many, many new wineries and new brands on the market and the subsequent dilution of so many old brands. There are about 140 new wineries in the Napa Valley alone. There are 480 in the state. We thought we needed a little PR. The competition is much stronger than it was seven or eight years ago, so we figured we had to do something to remind the people that we're still around and we thought these tastings of wine with food were one way of doing it.

We've gotten some data together but haven't had a chance to run it through a statistical analysis yet. It looks like we show some trends with regard to preferences of different wines with different foods.

We got excellent coverage by the press, especially the food writers. They thought that was great. Some wineries have cooking classes at their wineries, a few things like this. This is just our effort. We get together for other purposes but we don't really get together for promotion. Most people are pushing their own brand rather than have group advertising.

• • •

The new marketing accent on food-with-wine is just the most humorous thing that's hit me lately. Ever since wine has been made, for thousands of years, people have been drinking it with food. And now all of a sudden somebody says — somebody whose wine probably didn't do very well at tastings — well, we don't make our wine for tastings, we make it for drinking with food. And now everybody and his brother says "Our wine is for food." Well, what else is it for?

I get a big kick out of these promotion-type people. As soon as one comes up with an idea, everybody does the same thing. So "Our wine goes well with food" is the thing to do now. Well, what do you think I sell mine for? Table wine is all to be drunk with food and it always has been.

• • •

We want to make wine that *we* like, and our feeling is that wine should be compatible with food. We're not trying to make wines that are showy, necessarily. We want to win awards in fairs, but what's more important to us is that you can sit down with our wine, and it complements your meal.

The industry is so new. Maybe it was insecurity or maybe not knowing just exactly how to handle the grapes, but I think in the past people tried to make the most robust Cabernet they possibly could so you could beat your breast and say *Aha! This is a Cabernet!* The same with Chardonnay — the most alcoholic and intense flavor that you could have. But then when you taste a French wine — not that we're trying to imitate the French by any means — you realize that maybe they're not as great alone as they are with a meal. And with a *meal*, they're just exceptional.

I think that it's part of our maturing process as an industry that we're now — at least in the Napa Valley that's what I hear almost everyone say — we're not trying to make the biggest wine in the world, we're trying to make wine that complements a meal. And I think that's the future of wine.

• • •

It's always done by tasting, you know. The palate is the supreme test, and the customer's palate is the supreme test in the marketplace. And it's the customer's palate that's responsible for repeat sales. You can sell the first bottle, but if the customer doesn't like it, he may never buy a second. So the palate is the important thing.

A Code of Ethics

To those who enjoy a glass of wine with meals, there can be no connection between fine premium wine and the rotgut alcohol favored by derelicts on skid row. Thus, the following recent news item from the Associated Press rankled, especially since The Wine Institute had already adopted a voluntary Code of Advertising Standards in 1949, and strengthened it in 1978.

BAN SOUGHT ON BOOZE RADIO, TV COMMERCIALS

WASHINGTON—A public interest group called Monday for a ban or restrictions on wine and beer broadcast commercials to counteract what it says is a deliberate attempt by the alcoholic beverage industry to target advertising toward heavy drinkers and youths.

The Center for Science in the Public Interest, a non-profit consumer health organization founded by Ralph Nader, also urged a congressional investigation of alcohol marketing practices.

"The billion dollars that producers spend on advertising every year feeds America's No. 1 drug problem," said ... the Center's director. "Yet alcoholic beverages are marketed as if they were as wholesome as skim milk" ...

The Center recommended that:

Radio and TV advertising for beer and wine be banned or at least balanced by information about the harmful effects of alcohol.

All marketing efforts aimed at heavy drinkers, including alcoholics, and youths be halted.

Celebrities, whom youngsters might worship as heroes, not be allowed to appear in advertisements.

Print ads should contain health warnings and not associate drinking alcohol with success.

We have a code of ethics. Three points in that news story are outright lies about the wine business. Have you ever seen California wine ads on television? They're not aimed at heavy drinkers. That would be stupid. That's the surest way to get the Prohibitionists active. And celebrities or athletes — we don't use those in wine advertising. We don't need health warnings because wine is not unhealthy. And associating drinking with success. This is in our code too. We don't do that. Athletic success, or business success or anything. We advertise mainly that wine tastes good and it's healthy when properly used — when used with meals.

The following are the Guidelines of the Code of Advertising Standards of The Wine Institute generally adhered to by the wine industry throughout California.

1. A distinguishing and unique feature of wine is that it is traditionally served with meals or immediately before or following a meal. Therefore, when subscribers to this code use wine advertising which visually depicts a scene or setting where wine is to be served, such advertising shall include foods and show that they are available and being used or intended to be used.

   This guideline shall not apply to the depiction of a bottle of wine, vineyard, winery, label, professional tasting, etc., where emphasis is on the product.

2. Wine advertising should encourage the proper use of wine. Therefore, subscribers to this code shall not depict or describe in their advertising:

   a. The consumption of wine for the effects its alcohol content may produce.

   b. Direct or indirect reference to alcohol content or extra strength, except as otherwise required by law or regulation.

   c. Excessive drinking or persons who appear to have lost control or to be inappropriately uninhibited.

   d. Any suggestion that excessive drinking or loss of control is amusing or a proper subject for amusement.

   e. Any persons engaged in activities not normally associated with the moderate use of wine and a responsible life-style. Association of wine use in conjunction with feats of daring or activities requiring unusual skill is specifically prohibited.

   f. Wine in quantities inappropriate to the situation or inappropriate for moderate and responsible use.

3. Advertising of wine has traditionally depicted wholesome persons enjoying their lives and illustrating the role of wine in a mature lifestyle. Any attempt to suggest that wine directly contributes to success or achievement is unacceptable. Therefore, the following restrictions shall apply to

subscribers to this code:

a. Wine shall not be presented as being essential to personal performance, social attainment, achievement, success or wealth.

b. The use of wine shall not be directly associated with social, physical or personal problem solving.

c. Wine shall not be presented as vital to social acceptability and popularity or as the key factor in such popularity.

d. It shall not be suggested that wine is crucial for successful entertaining.

4. Any advertisement which has particular appeal to persons below the legal drinking age is unacceptable. Therefore, wine advertising by code subscribers shall not:

a. Show models and personalities in advertisements who appear to be under 25 years of age.

b. Use music, language, gestures or cartoon characters specifically associated with or directed toward those below the legal drinking age.

c. Appear in children's or juveniles' magazines, newspapers, television programs, radio programs or other media specifically oriented to persons below the legal drinking age.

d. Be presented as being related to the attainment of adulthood or associated with "rites of passage" to adulthood.

e. Suggest that a wine product resembles or is similar to another type of beverage or product (milk, soda, candy) having particular appeal to persons below the legal drinking age.

f. Use traditional heroes of the young such as those engaged in pastimes and occupations having a particular appeal to persons below the legal drinking age. (For example, cowboys, race car drivers, rock stars, etc.)

g. Use amateur or professional sports celebrities, past or present.

5. Code subscribers shall not show motor vehicles in such a way as to suggest that they are to be operated in conjunction with wine use. Advertising should in no way suggest that wine be used in connection with driving.

6. Wine advertising by code subscribers shall not appear in or directly adjacent to television or radio programs or print media which dramatize or glamorize over-consumption or inappropriate use of alcoholic beverages.

7. Wine advertising by code subscribers shall make no reference to wine's medicinal values.

8. Wine advertising by code subscribers shall not degrade the image or status of any ethnic, minority or other group.

9. Wine advertising by code subscribers shall not exploit the human form, feature provocative or enticing poses nor be demeaning to any individual.

All advertising — including, but not limited to direct mail, point-of-sale, outdoor displays, radio, television and print media — should adhere to both the letter and the spirit of the above code.

Labeling Wine

The Bureau of Alcohol, Tobacco and Firearms [BATF], an arm of the U.S. Treasury Department, must approve every label design before it can be used on wine bottles. A black and white photostat of the label to be printed is submitted by the winery for preliminary approval. Then, if the winery is a member of the Wine Institute, the label is usually sent to them to be looked over before being forwarded to the government for final approval.

Our label is my artwork. That's one of the places we saved a good deal of money. One of our colleagues has a new label — they did need one, for sure. Apparently it cost 20,000 dollars to develop. Ours cost me a bottle of ink and time. And a tired wrist. The development of the label in the end didn't cost more than a hundred dollars. I don't think there's another winery that can say that. And it's a nice label. There are some that clearly look home done, but ours has some sophistication to it.

We followed BATF to the letter. We designed it with the 1983 regulations in mind so we didn't have to change anything. In a way it was limiting. Anytime you have to do the appellation in the same size type as the varietal — right there that's an esthetic decision that's already been made for you. In a way it's challenging. You can do anything you want, but these few things.

• • •

It certainly inhibits the creative part of wine packaging, and there's things like ... they keep talking about ingredient labeling that has to be either on the face of the label or the back. There's a number of different regulations that will be coming in. The BATF regulations are that thick. You can't even make sense of them.

• • •

You go into so much hassle and debate about what you should name yourself. We finally came up with our name. Then we phoned certain artists and asked if they could come up with a label, and they'd start telling us this is what you should be naming yourself. That was more input than we really wanted from them. Also they weren't willing to come up with a number of labels for us to choose from. We all have certain different ideas and we like to have a good argument over what label we'd like.

For a while we got quite discouraged, and this friend who is very knowledgeable about wines asked to do it. He came up with about eight labels that went from the most austere, maybe traditional French style, and this was probably the other extreme. What we liked about it is that the design just seemed to flow, and it felt good to us. It's a label that's unusual and it makes people take a stand, I think, whether you like it or not.

• • •

There's another set of regulations for labeling, and that sort of thing. We don't go in for vineyard designations, which we feel is just a marketing ploy really, unless you have an unusual vineyard that produces a very complete, complex wine.

We're great believers in blending. In '78 and '79 we did a Pinot Noir from the same vineyard for both years. We don't usually blend two vintages together, but in this case it made the best wine.

So we applied for a label to the BATF that had the exact percentages of '78 and of '79. That's telling the consumer exactly what is in that bottle. The BATF would not allow us to use it. They would not allow us to put those percentages, to put the two years. You can do it if it's sold only in California, but not if it's sold in the rest of the country.

So we applied for a label that said in a French phrase — *assemblage de deux vins qui se complement* — that the wine was a blend of two vintages. It was a classy little thing to do for a wine that was sold as a vintage wine. The words are similar enough that you can figure it out if you don't know French. We did it in French because if you put that on the label in English, it would have looked kind of crass and lose all its romantic appeal.

And they sent that back and said, "We speak French, you know." So we said, "We assumed you speak French, or we would have sent you a translation." They ended up letting us use the French phrase that said it is a blend of two wines, but we could not even hint to the consumer that there were two different years. So it went out with the least amount of information.

The Wine Institute had encouraged us to go ahead and blend it, and challenge the BATF label, because they had been trying to get this dealt with and they had never got a response from the BATF explaining why they took this position. Well, we finally did get a response. The response was "It's not in the regs." It wasn't in the regulations.

An Interview with:

Two Label Specialists

The interview that follows is a composite of a conversation with Sebastian Titus and Wesley Poole, two well-known Napa Valley graphic artists who specialize in wine art. This adjunct of industry promotion and marketing strategy is of sufficient importance to support several such artists in the area.

The interview took place in the reception area of their busy, pleasant studio shortly before a client was to decide on the label for a wine yet to be produced. Two dozen empty wine bottles of the traditional form for Sauvignon Blanc, each bearing a mockup of a different label design, were arranged on a low circular table surrounded by comfortable — but not too comfortable — chairs. The presentation would be of the utmost seriousness, because an attractive label is often responsible for the sale of a bottle of wine.

We formed our studio to specialize in the wine industry. Over the past several years in the Napa Valley we have developed a very clear knowledge of the wine-buying public and the wine-producing public. All of our work is basically wine-oriented. It's just a matter of paying your dues and having a successful track record. A lot of our labels are very old and have done very well on the shelf.

Our expertise is how to package wine, not just a simple piece of paper on the bottle, but developing the total image or mystique of the winery for the public. Being aware of those things is the reason we attract the kind of work that we do, which is pretty much the top end. People who buy premium wines buy less than five percent of the total wine consumed in this country, and those are the people that we're trying to get through to on a boutique level.

Corporate wineries are something else entirely. There's a number of major studios in San Francisco that have a huge design business and they do heavy corporate accounts. A wine label would be something that they would do merely occasionally and they would do it for a *big* winery and it's lots and lots of money. They've done some interesting labels. Their fees and just the whole environment is larger than ours — not that they do more successful work. I would say any other large studio in California would like to do labels, and some of them in their portfolios will have one or two labels. Some wineries go to New York. Some do their own labels — you can usually tell, because they're usually the ones that are crummy.

When you're getting into mass market, you're dealing with a different type of buyer, a different profile, but with the boutique buyers, the premium wine buyers, we know what flies. We know from experience and from a sort of gut feeling what will work and won't. With the very small wineries the label can very often be the only connection to the wine buying public. They don't have brochures, they don't have posters or point-of-sale pieces, and they do no advertising per se — they can't afford it, the buying doesn't merit it. So the package becomes very important. If a winery goes to a designer who has never done a label, they're just risking everything in a big way. Basically there are too many small wineries, and they won't all make it.

We get new business through reputation. It's a good example of how word of mouth works in the industry. It's sort of an internal kind of thing and once you've earned your stripes, you become a part of the inner circle. I don't think a lot of advertising would do us any good.

There's no school to go to, there's not even one particular place to go to learn. Anyone wanting to get into wine packaging could only be able to do it through experience, over a period of time working with a studio like ours. There's no other way.

After awhile you just start to get a feel for what the wine industry's all about. Of course, we make an effort.

We read all the publications, and go to various events. We talk to winery people all the time and we're out there, so it gives us a huge advantage over anybody else who's trying to make wine labels.

Our first and foremost job is to come up with something that sells wine, and we won't do a label that doesn't sell wine. It's just as simple as that. But the other half of what we do is trying to deal with the client, and take their personalities and egos and sometimes peculiar preferences and all of that into consideration.

It's becoming obvious to a lot of people that the wine business *is* a business these days, but still a lot of people on the premium end enter into it for very personal, romantic reasons. A lot of them are very talented, very enjoyable people, but they tend to be very strong-willed. We spend a lot of time convincing certain people what will work, because we know. But there again that's our job and that's where experience comes in.

Our customers are certainly more aware of wine than the average wine-drinker, or they wouldn't get into the business. There are exceptions to that rule though. Sometimes someone who doesn't have a vast amount of wine knowledge wants to get into it. They think they're going to make a lot of money, or they enjoy it for some other aspect — maybe it's a 40-acre estate in the Valley or some other reason — and their wine knowledge might not be as good as it could be.

Theoretically (gesturing toward the presentation), any one of these labels would work for either a light Sauvignon Blanc or an intense Sauvignon Blanc. We usually taste the wine before we do the labels. Winemaking considerations are not really part of our business, unless we taste a wine that we think might not sell. We might offer that opinion, but it really isn't our business.

From a personal standpoint, it's always nice to know the winery is making *good* wine because then you get more enthusiastic. In good conscience, if we feel somebody's going to totally fail, we tell them so. We're busy.

We don't need the work that badly.

On this one, it's more talking with the winery people of the style they want to make, because this wine does not yet exist. That's usually the case for a new winery. They don't have any wine to sell yet — it's in the barrel or not ready for release. Most of the time there are ways of tasting them. We have tasted the wines from their vineyards from other people.

If a client is doing a very particular, almost a specialty wine, say a Sauvignon Blanc with a very high alcohol, very intense etcetera etcetera, that would become part of the considerations in doing the label, but if it's a wine that's within the sort of accepted scope, it's more important to latch onto something at the winery. The style of wine is a secondary consideration. More than the label matching the style of wine, it's the style of wine matching the market.

We're one of the few studios that does a presentation for a prospective client in this manner, with a lot of different approaches that look printed, but are really hand-done. It's a very accurate presentation. Most initial concepts are done on tissues. Just rough sketches sort of, and then when they get some direction from the client any top studio before the label is printed would go into this kind of process and do them more or less as finished as the state of the art allows without actually printing the label. In some cases the label is actually done as a press proof, actually printed in a very small quantity to make sure that everything — color and so forth — is right and then they go into a bigger press run for the actual label.

Basically, we're specialized, although we step out occasionally in jams and olive oil. By specializing we can offer expertise that if we were broad-based as a small studio we couldn't do. There's only so much time in the day.

It's quite an adventure. Like every other aspect of the wine industry, it's much more complex these days than it used to be.

Wine and the Outside World

Wine Snobs and Wine Writers

As interest in wine on the part of the general public increases, that social phenomenon known as the wine snob may be on the way out. Much of the credit for this belongs to wine writers, for sharing their knowledge and enthusiasm with the rest of us.

Compared to the number of people who drink wine today versus 20 years ago, there are fewer wine snobs. When there weren't many people drinking wine, there were basically two types: the wine snobs who drank the imported wines and oohed and aahed, and the bums who couldn't afford more expensive alcohol, so they drank sweet wine.

As more and more people are drinking wine, the middle group — the average sensible American — is coming to it, and he's neither a bum nor a snob. There are still a few wine snobs left who will buy a wine just because it's expensive, but percentagewise there are very few now, I'm happy to report. I think some winos still exist, but I don't think that's my fault. Anyway, the percentage is getting less on that end of the scale, too.

• • •

There's always the person who's going to order the most expensive bottle of champagne on a restaurant wine list or the most expensive bottle in a retail shop just so he can serve the most expensive bottle, but I think people are becoming much more aware of values and that a fine glass of wine is to be served every night, and eliminating a lot of this quote "snob appeal". It's still in effect in some areas of the country where wine consumption is still new, but I would venture to say that in the next decade this entire country will eliminate this snob appeal.

If someone wants to buy a fine Bordeaux or California Cabernet and it happens to be the finest of the vintage, they're going to have to pay for it, because there's only a limited supply of that particular wine, but certainly to indiscriminately go out and buy it just because it's the most expensive ... I think the more knowledge a consumer has, the less likely he is to do that. Or she. *One* is.

• • •

I think some wine writers have a tendency to convey a snobbish image, but they have to write about things that are interesting or no one's going to read them. Wine writers do this, but on the other hand they continue to constantly whet the appetite of the wine consumers and I think that's as important as any other aspect of the wine business, to keep people's curiosity about wines ticking. So they definitely serve a positive purpose.

I often think that most wine writers are just writing articles for the same people, over and over, and it's a shame that someone doesn't try to write columns which are geared more to people who are just learning about the basics of wine, and to try to instill in them the idea that wine is just a simple beverage to be consumed with food. The only one that comes to mind right now who is kind of like that is Jerry Mead, who writes to the common man, the person who wants to know a little bit more about wine to be able to buy some well-priced wine to drink night after night and not have to spend a small king's ransome for a bottle.

• • •

Wine writers have done an awful lot for this industry, because they've made the consumer aware that there is such a product as wine.

On the other side of that coin, there are probably people who have received, in a much undeserved fashion, comments from wine writers who know little or nothing about what they are talking about, and some poor devil trying to get his product up got shot down on the first round.

I can turn that one around too, and tell you that I feel that if the little guy makes some good wines, he should get praise for it. They should be honestly evaluated. If he makes bad ones, he should get kicked, too. I want to be treated the same way.

• • •

Wine snobbery seems to be at about the same level as a few years ago, and it's the same type of thing. I don't think there's more wine snobbery now. I think there are more wine snobs. More people are interested in wine — some people get a little carried away.

We had a blind tasting here with about 16 different wines and we discussed them afterwards. It was sort of like a class. I have a friend who's a wine-buyer for one of the stores, and she's very basic and down-to-earth. One of the other persons at the tasting said, quote "I think this wine has a *modern* taste".

People seemed to accept it, sort of nodding and going on with what they were doing. And then my buyer friend said "What the hell is a modern taste?" Everyone had to stop to think about that one.

People get into descriptions that don't communicate. They get into all of these wine terms or start making up their own.

• • •

Winemakers will talk in the same general language that wine writers write in, but they are more specific and not so romantic. If I'm talking to one of my colleagues or one of my friends up the road, I don't tell him that this wine reminds me of berries or pickles and raw pineapples along with a few apples thrown in, with maybe an aftertaste of sausage or something like that. I think that the winemakers may say "It has an oxydized nose, a very fruity nose, or a grapey nose, or this reminds me of a pineapple character ... "

I don't mean to criticize some of these wine writers and some of their terms, because I think that whether we are wine writers or wine makers, we're all searching for the descriptive words for wine. That's what it's all about.

Fairs and Tastings

Competitive tastings and wine fairs are important to the marketing of wine, because from these come the lists of prizewinners that consumers often take with them when they buy.

For a while there we weren't really going to fairs at all because we didn't think much of the overall way they were doing the judging and so on, and there wasn't all that much competition out there. But now there's more competition and a lot of people are paying attention to awards won at fairs, so we've decided to go in, and whatever we win, we win.

• • •

Sure we're in fairs. All the time. Not international. Basically the Los Angeles, Sonoma County Harvest Fair, and the Orange County Fair and sometimes the *San Jose Mercury News*. In the Orange County Fair, the judges are wine people — winemakers. The Los Angeles Fair is mostly wine writers, and in the Sonoma County Harvest Fair there are wine writers and technical people also; it's a cross section. We're basically doing it to see how we're standing up to our peers—other wineries. Any more than that is superfluous, it's overkill.

We basically enter just to see how we're doing, and if you win a gold medal it's just great on the marketing end of it, but mainly it just keeps you humble.

We've won a lot of gold medals. You submit a wine that's very good, and it doesn't win anything, so you go out and taste it against wines that do win things, and in many instances the wines that win things are good or better than your particular wine and in some instances you come away thinking "My wine is still better than the gold medal wine, but the judges didn't think so . . . ." It's an educational tool for us.

• • •

Way back before the turn of the century, the first

international competition that California wine may have been in was in 1889, I think it was, a Paris Exposition, and some California wines including some Napa Valley wines were there, and the Napa Valley wines took very high positions in judging at that time. Then in 1900 there was another famous world fair with wine judging involved in it and California wines gave a kind of repeat performance. The thing of gaining recognition has been going on for almost a century, and we've not reached the end of the line yet.

Some of the most sensational — in the way of attracting the attention of the wine world to the high quality of California wines — of these international winetasting competitions have been set up only by a couple of individuals. Steven Spurriur, and Englishman in the wine business, originated a tasting in Paris that rocked the whole wine world in about 1974 or '75. He had a sales organization in Paris, and it was he who decided to put on a wine competition that pitted some of the finest California wines against some of the very finest French wine. I think his entire panel of judges was all French, but they tasted blind, without knowing which wine they were tasting. The California wines took about eight out of ten of the First Places.

Some of the French thought it was crazy. Some thought it was a joke — a dream, it never happened, you know. But then the same thing has been repeated at other competitions and judgings in more recent years.

• • •

There are more judgings conducted by personal wine writers than there are state fairs all put together. I don't care whether it's the Los Angeles County Fair, the Orange County Fair or whatever, the fact remains that a lot of the wine writers are making judgments today which they're putting into print. And let's face it. They are a very powerful influence on the consumer. If you write that this wine, to you, has a very pleasing character, a very pleasant fruit, it has a nice so-called finish or aftertaste, and that goes into a wine writer's column or on a sheet given to a retailer, that has a lot to do with the purchasing.

I'm sure there are a lot of people who go into the stores with their little list and say somebody recommended this, and let me see what they've got.

There's nothing wrong with that. God! How can you go into a store ... ? Suppose all the Chardonnays are on the shelf? There are 160 of them! If it did happen, I just hope they picked up one of mine first.

• • •

What's so misleading about winning awards — the L.A. County Fair, the Orange County fair — is that what gets awarded is not necessarily the wine that goes best with a meal, but rather the wine that sticks out. So a lot of people will make wines that will do well in a fair, that a little bit of sugar is left in them, or that have a little more alcohol, a little more wood — something that makes them stand out. But you take it apart from that tasting, it might not be the wine that you'd pick to have with dinner that night.

The San Francisco Fair just started last year. They had a wine competition that Harvey Steiman organized. I was thrilled at that fair because his whole philosophy was let's not reward the wine that necessarily sticks out at the expense of the wine that may be more delicate. He instructed all the people who were his tasting board to go back and taste those wines that may have been overshadowed. Sure, pick out your favorites, but go back. Was maybe this wine overshadowed because it was between two great big blockbusters? Pull that wine out and taste that again. The wines that were awarded in that fair seemed to be a little better balanced overall. I felt that was a real step in the right direction in terms of giving an award for the wine.

• • •

Vertical tasting is the same variety of wine over a period of years — say a Chardonnay from '78, '79, '80, '81, and '82 out of the barrel. It gives an excellent example, particularly if the winery has been consistent in its stylistic approach. It's a very good example of vintage differences and in aging potential.

● ● ●

I have a lot of good friends who are wine writers, and they're doing a good job. But it's very, very difficult for me to give credibility to a person who says, "I sat down and tasted 25 wines of X variety and these are my comments", because I immediately pray to God that he tasted mine first or second and not Number 23 at the end of the line.

● ● ●

At tastings, if you're going to have 25 wines, it's fair to be at the end of the line if you're not swallowing them all. Everybody's different. I've seen people at tastings who don't spit the wine out. That's the way they operate, and it works for them. I've never smoked in my life. I don't see how people that smoke taste wine — I've heard that it's very difficult, but I know a very well-known enologist who smokes, who stopped smoking, and the minute he stopped smoking he lost his palate — couldn't taste the wine any more. So for him, it fit to smoke and to continue to smoke. Some tasters can take 25 little sips and still say at the end that a wine has a nose. They say they can.

At a tasting I tried taking 25 little sips, and I was OK until about Number 17 or 18. Interestingly enough, I could really tell I lost it. I was in agreement with people that I really agree with on wines until toward the last seven. We compared our notes and scores, and I was just completely off.

What I'll do at a tasting sometimes is I'll skip around, because sometimes psychologically ... I always like to number them A-B-C rather than 1-2-3, because at a lot of tastings you give points. At all of the tastings I do I always letter the wines, because you'll pick the wine that's first, and that's your Number 1, your A choice. Or sometimes we'll just do the two or three wines we like the best and the wine we like the least.

And if you're really seriously tasting wines, you should spit a lot out. You shouldn't swallow it. For one thing, when you get into numbers, you lose your palate after so many. You can't taste 25 wines and swallow each one, even the kind you sip. You will just get blotto. It's not just that you become inebriated, which a lot of people can take 25 little sips and not be, but that you don't taste the wine.

● ● ●

If you go and watch a blind tasting, or people who are really concentrating on their wines, they'll go through a series of wines and just sniff them and write volumes about what they smell.

The next step is if that wine doesn't fulfill the expectations created by the smell, it's rated down, because that's part and parcel of a good wine. Your anticipation from smelling it should be followed through on by taste.

The Gewurztraminer is an example of wines that are difficult to do that with. Frequently, particularly in a dry Gewurztraminer, you smell all this floral, fruity, spicy sweetness, and then you get this bitter wine. It's a very jarring experience, so there should be that follow-through.

● ● ●

More and more people are becoming acquainted with wine and enjoying it as a beverage of moderation. They're using it more and more with their meals, but they're not using it fast enough for me. And that's because of our background. We were not brought up on wine. We are not a wine-conscious country.

Thousands of people want to come to wine tastings. They're interested in wine, and this is what we want. I just spent some time on the road, going around holding tasting seminars. And we're not the only ones to do that. There are an awful lot of people doing that today to bring attention to their product, but I think we have a long way to go.

We talk about the great consumption of wines in France and Italy and Argentina, but you have to remember they've been making wine, working with wine, for maybe a couple of thousand years, and we've been working with it a couple of hundred years. You don't get somebody to switch over from milk to wine in five or ten years.

An Interview with:

Publishers of a Wine Newsletter

Any lingering doubts in the reader's mind that wine is a serious enterprise would be likely to evaporate during a chat with Charles Olken and Earl Singer, writers, editors and publishers of one of the most widely distributed wine review services in the world.

Subscribers say they respect Connoisseurs' Guide to California Wines *because it offers a full range of criticism. Besides lauding wines that deserve acclaim, and telling why they think so, Olken and Singer do not hesitate to condemn premium offerings better ignored. In this case, their succinct opinions and the reasons therefor are followed by the starkly uncompromising, probably devastating, graphic symbol of a wineglass turned upside down.*

We met with portly, mustachioed Olken and intense, Velasquez-bearded Singer late of a dark Alameda night at the publication's headquarters. The talk never veered from the subject — the why and how of their wine reviews — and the refreshment served was strong, serious black coffee.

In the '60s California wine had revived to the point of being interesting enough to attract lots of attention. Up until then, only a few insiders were collectors, because the upscale, high visibility side of great wines had been European.

We were living here, working in San Francisco. We knew that something exciting was happening, yet nothing was being published to serve the connoisseur collecter interested in California wines.

We started our newsletter not as industry professionals in the Masters of Winemaking sense, but as interested, dedicated consumers who felt we had something valuable to say about California wine to people like ourselves.

We decided *Connoisseurs' Guide* should be what we ourselves were looking for in a wine publication and couldn't find elsewhere — how to choose the best wines and how to use them with food. We felt that quality level, availability of wine in the marketplace, broad — not specific — categories of food that an individual wine might go with, and whether a wine is for current drinking or would be better with further aging was what people like ourselves wanted to find out about.

Our magazine is very personal, because it is done very much to satisfy our own curiosity. We review wines for people in the trade, but mainly for people who find the number of wines available kind of baffling and might be disappointed with a randomly chosen bottle.

We took our idea on the road, as it were, in the fall of 1974. We printed an issue, took out a couple of ads and sent some flyers, and people started sending us money, which indicated there were people out there interested in a serious publication about California wine.

From the day we felt there was an opportunity to the day the first issue appeared, we spent something like ten months designing and redesigning the format of the newsletter, and designing tasting forms.

There are tasting forms and tasting methods geared to

point scores. We feel that wine doesn't add up to points. It adds up to certain experiences through the senses, and we wanted our newsletter to talk about the wines we taste the way people would experience them.

Ours is a very elaborate form that's like taking an exam, in that we ask tasters to describe their reactions in detail, rather than check items off and assign them points.

Each of our tastings will normally involve people who can bring various perspectives on wine — a winemaker or two, one or more retailers and restaurateurs, and others experienced in tasting wine who can taste with some consistency and can express themselves. They must also be willing to sit with us through a fairly demanding blind tasting that involves retasting and discussing each wine.

We ask the people who taste with us to concentrate on different aspects of the wine — aromas, feel on the palate, flavors, aftertaste, balance — but the work really begins *after* we get their comments. Then we have to figure out what it all means, and write a tasting note that will communicate to our subscribers the characteristics of the wine. The ultimate test of *Connoisseurs' Guide* or of any wine publication is the reaction people have when they pull the cork on a bottle we've recommended. We work very hard so that when we write something and someone pulls a cork, they won't disagree with us.

We probably taste 4,000 wines a year, and write about 2,000, because we taste a lot of wine we don't write about — older wines, or wines in wineries from the barrel and at presentations. Almost all the wines we write about we taste in comparison to other wines or in blind tastings where we don't know what the wine is. If we vary from the pattern, such as reviewing wines shown at the Napa Valley Wine Library, then we say so.

We retaste a large number of the wines we write about. We particularly retaste every wine that we have *not* liked to make sure that there wasn't a particular reaction against a bottle, or its location in a tasting, or any other random factor that would cause the tasters to say they didn't like that *wine*, when they didn't like that particular *bottle*. This happened recently with a Chardonnay from a reputable winery with their Private Reserve — their expensive Chardonnay — and no one liked it. We opened up a second bottle, and it was the same. Then you know that you have a wine that is flawed. It's the only way you'd know.

At this point, having tasted probably 40 or 50,000 different bottles of wine over the last eight or nine years, we don't think we have any biases that would make us favor one winery over another. We've reached the point where if it shows itself in the blind tasting, it's a good wine, and if it doesn't, it isn't, because that's the method by which we do our research. Besides, our focus is on *wines*, not wineries.

Our tastings last all evening. We begin about 6:30, and go through two sets of eight wines very carefully. No one in the tasting knows which bottles are there. And if one of us sets up the tasting, the other won't know what's in it. Typically, our wives cover the bottles, or if we put the covering on, somebody else puts the lettering on. Anyway, we make sure we don't know where a wine is located.

We'll taste the wines blind, in quiet, everyone concentrating and writing notes, and then each person will come up with a preference order. Then we add up the rank order of that particular set. We use rankings as a way of developing a conversation about that wine, so the tasters will say *why* they prefer one wine to another. In this way we end up with an *understanding* of that wine, and how to communicate that to our subscribers.

We're looking for many views of the elephant so that we can describe a wine in a way our readers can understand. There are a lot of different tastes in wine, and what we're trying to do is describe a wine so that people looking for different tastes can find them, and find exactly what they're searching for.

We evolved the system we did of limiting the number of wines we taste at each tasting, and involving people beyond ourselves, because with all our experience in this business, neither of us feels we have the perfect palate. Nor have we ever met it.

The perfect palate would describe every wine tasted in a manner so that everybody else in the room says "Yes, that's exactly right, that's exactly what I'm tasting. That describes the wine." The perfect palate would never make mistakes, never go off on a tangent, never pick up on something in the wine and say "I really hated that aspect" and mark the wine all the way down, and have everybody else come back with "You called that aspect volatile acidity, but what I really think you have here is some overstated American oak, and you've missed it."

Wine is very complicated stuff. People are imperfect. You can get very hung up on keying in on a particular aroma or a particular sensation and then construct in your mind a whole scenario that is perfectly consistent with what you focussed on. No one else in the room is going to pick that up, and you've tricked yourself into being completely in left field.

After the tasting, we usually test a wine for residual sugar, for acid, pH, and on occasions where we're really baffled, we'll send it off to a lab for testing because we want to make sure that we're not ascribing a chemical characteristic, or a complex chemical element, that isn't there.

One of the reasons it helps to have winemakers at these tastings is that they're trained chemists, whereas we are consumers. If the professionals are disagreeing, the way to get the answer is to send the wine off to a lab for any specialized tests that require heating and distillation.

One test that winemakers like to run themselves in the winery lab is for volatile acidity, which is really vinegar, because that's a flaw that you can taste and that at a certain level becomes unpleasant. Sometimes one winemaker will say, "This is beyond the legal limit for vinegar in wines." And the other guy will say "I can't taste it. I don't think it's there. That's just American oak." They want to find out who's right, out of curiosity and professional pride.

While we often have professionals at our tastings, we decided right from the beginning, to protect them and to protect us, never to have a winemaker taste his own wine. If he ends up liking it and everyone else hates it, or the opposite, it's embarrassing all around. Besides, we don't want people playing guessing games with the wine.

For us, blind tasting of finished wine is the only reliable method. From a marvelous barrel or tank of wine, there are all sorts of steps before it reaches the consumer, and you can react very positively to a tank or a barrel sample. You taste the same wine months later, and after it's been bottled, it's really not the same wine. Sometimes it's close, and sometimes it is so far off that you question your senses. We're interested in what's going to reach the consumer, so we don't do previews of wines any more.

And we don't do in-winery tastings any more. Wine always tastes better in a winery or at dinner than it does in blind tasting, simply because the setting is entirely positive. When you taste in a winery, chances are you're tasting with the owner or the winemaker. You're at the winery, out in wine country. That is bound to influence your critical faculties.

To round up the wines for our tastings, we start out with a shopping list, and put in about 3,000 miles a month driving to about 40 stores in the greater Bay Area searching for the wine to buy at retail.

There's nothing ethically incorrect about tasting wines that wineries send you, or ethically incorrect about wineries' sending their products around, but from our standpoint, we feel it's appropriate to buy as many wines at retail as we can, because then there can't be a question in anybody's mind about whether or not we've been sent a ringer or whether or not we're tasting some peoples' wines and not others. In essence, we have scoured the market, so we can pretty well say that what we're tasting is representative of the wine available in the marketplace.

Availability is one of the difficult issues in the wine business, because it's easy for people to start small wineries. The numbers of small producers in California have added vitality to the industry, but often what they produce is not widely available. They're also why there's four or five hundred Chardonnays and why somebody has to taste 3,000 wines a year the average person can't get around to.

At every tasting we serve a dinner oriented to that particular type of wine so that we have a chance to check it with food. With Cabernet Sauvignon, for example, it might take 20 different tastings before we get to the point where we're finished, so we get a chance to taste Cabernet with 20 different dishes. We develop a sense of what kinds of foods go with various Cabernet Sauvignons, and that becomes part of the input to our writing process.

It has become trendy to call some wines "food wines", as if drinking wine with food is some kind of new discovery. Often the term has been bastardized to mean that even though the wine doesn't have a great deal of character, if you drink it with food, maybe you won't notice. Lord knows if you have a fresh piece of salmon in a hollandaise sauce, a light wine is going to go away and hide in a corner, and this so-called food wine is going to be no wine at all. The best California wines have always been food wines. That's not a discovery of the '80s.

One learns about wine with food in a variety of ways —from people who know more, by reading, by listening, and by experience. One of our worst combinations *ever* involved a Petite Sirah — a big, gutsy red wine we thought should go with spaghetti. A similar Petite Sirah went wonderfully with red meat not more than two weeks before, and we thought we could serve it with this nice, rich, red sauce. But the sweet edge of the tomatoes made this particular Petite Sirah taste like dust. The flavor went away, and all you were left was the feeling of the tannin in your mouth and there was no wine.

We never, ever saw written in a book "Petite Sirah is great with roast beef, but beware using it with spaghetti." That's something you have to learn on your own.

Serving Wine

Wine people agree on one rule: Wine should be served just the way you like it. Your palate is the one true guide. After that, there are individual rules for the use and enjoyment of wine about which feeling occasionally runs strong.

My rule for using wine is just use common sense. To match this specific wine at 62.5 degrees Fahrenheit with this specific chicken cooked that way, of course not. You don't drink a big, heavy, rich Cabernet Sauvignon with a light, delicate fillet of sole, or if you've got a good piece of prime, rare roast beef, you don't pull out a simple Johannisberg Riesling to go with that. But basically, red wine, red meat, white wine with fish is a good — not rule, guideline. We usually serve white wine with chicken or fish, and of course we like Cabernet with lamb. Almost any good wine goes well with any good food. But you follow your own taste. It's just common sense.

As for chilling, we don't do it. We just chill the Chardonnay maybe 30 minutes in the refrigerator and the Johannisberg Riesling more. Definitely Chardonnay should be less chilled. The colder something is, the more subdued the flavors and certainly the aromas. The aromas are volatile, and the more you chill something, the less evaporation you're going to get. Wine is something we enjoy by nose more than by mouth. Unfortunately, restaurants have just one refrigerator and they put all the wines in there.

• • •

I like to drink my wine so I can taste it, so I don't usually refrigerate my whites. I bring them out of our cellar — a little cooler than room temperature, but certainly not cold. The colder the wine is, the more you mask things, and a lot of flaws are masked. If I'm drinking a jug wine, I'll drink it cold because there's a lot of things I maybe don't want to taste in the wine. When we go to a restaurant and they bring the bucket and that wine is chilled, I yank it out of there immediately and put it on the table so it'll warm up so I can taste it and smell it.

• • •

For us the one great rule is glasses. We are just horrified at retail shops with wine bars that will pour wine in plastic cups. Wine glasses are designed with a purpose — the enjoyment of wine. This is not snobbery. It's not frivolous. The champagne glass that you see at all these weddings — now that's frivolous. A true champagne glass is the tall fluted kind, and the reason for that is that you want a minimum of exposure, because it keeps the bubbles. In fact, what they do frequently is score them at the bottom at the center, because the bubbles are encouraged by that scoring to keep coming up, but if you have that big flat open surface, all the bubbles dissipate immediately and you've got a glass of flat champagne. Not to mention how difficult it is to hold those things.

Another thing: Wine glasses are not supposed to be filled to the top. The purpose of the design is so you can swirl the glass and put your nose in and take a deep breath, and get all the bouquet and aroma from the wine. You swirl it and watch what's called the legs. You can see a number of heavy droplets. That gives you some idea of the thickness, the viscosity, of the wine. A thin wine is going to come down in a thin sheet. It won't have legs. If you fill the glass, you can't swirl it, and when you put your nose to it, you don't get all that. Frequently the best part of wine is smelling it, so for glasses you look for that nice round swirling motion.

This is an absolutely perfect glass for even red wine. It's not bad for champagne either. Frequently for heavier reds they'll have a bigger goblet type that you fill even lower because those are harder to swirl and will come shooting out of the glass. Reds have a richer, heavier aroma. You need all that space to capture that.

One of our biggest pet peeves is to go into a restaurant

and they'll pour our wine to the top, and we've just gotten it drunk down low enough so we can swirl it and enjoy it and we turn our backs and before we know it, it's filled up to the top again.

That's a tipoff on how sophisticated a restaurant is with wine serving. Nowadays most fine restaurants have people who know how to serve wine, but, depending on their clientele, restaurants are in a very tough spot. A number of customers are insulted if they don't get a full glass of wine.

• • •

The only rule that I have is always to serve wine with food. Alcohol is something that, used correctly, is a wonderful thing, and abusing it is a very terrible thing to do. People shouldn't drink alcohol on an empty stomach. The lightest of wines will go to your head if you don't eat something with it — that's the nature of alcohol. Even at tastings they usually have breads and things like cheese and bread. If you're just having wine and not a meal, you ought to have some munchies, or a little cheese and crackers, or if you're into cooking, some nice little hors d'oeuvres that go well with wine.

I just can't imagine a good meal without wine. I always drink wine with dinner. It's unfair to the food not to serve good wine.

"A perfect wine glass — not bad for champagne, either."

100 Recipes
That Go with Wine

The very special recipes that follow are an exquisite mix. Many are the favorites of generations of winery families, sent by the son or daughter who functions as Marketing Manager. A few are the creations of chefs of international reputation or of winery culinary scholarship recipients, and some have been the object of study in classes, seminars, and workshops at the wineries. Some are designed by credentialed cooks who follow the new career of Wine and Food Consultant and work for wineries in much the same way as do label designers, with the same end in view: to show off wines to best advantage.

All of them demonstrate that the same pride, care, and dedication that goes into the making of premium wine also goes into the creation of recipes to complement that wine.

Where the recipe is for a side dish, the contributor often omitted wine serving suggestions, because any wine chosen would be for the complete menu. In such cases, we did not presume to fill the gap. In following wine serving suggestions, the reader should bear in mind all the style variations possible in one varietal wine.

Because we wanted to keep this book as non-"commercial" as possible, we have listed the wineries' own suggestions without trademark or year. With each recipe is the name of the winery that supplied it, and of course each would prefer that its own wines be used.

In this connection, we must mention two exceptions to our intention not to name names:

According to a consultant, there are two different kinds of Muscat. One is essentially a lighter table wine, always under 14 percent alcohol, whether sweet or dry. Then there is a heavier, richer Muscat fortified with brandy at about 20 percent alcohol. For this reason, we have opted to leave references to Muscat exactly as they came from the winery.

Also, in the present strong market for white wines over red, some wineries have begun to use unusual names for Vin Rosé, such as Pinot Noir Blanc, White Zinfandel, White Cabernet, and other fancies, so when in doubt, we have left these proprietary names as is.

And now, the recipes — compliments of the Chef!

Appetizers

PUNCH   Heitz Wine Cellars

Put one frozen apricot in a champagne glass. Add one ounce Southern Comfort. Fill glass with chilled champagne.

"A great 4th of July drink for a brunch."

MUSCAT MIMOSA   Sutter Home Winery

Blend together one 12-ounce can frozen orange juice and one bottle chilled Muscat Amabile. Add 12 ounces club soda. Stir. Serve over ice cubes, if desired.

BRANDIED CHEESE FONDUE   Sterling Vineyards

    ½ cup flour
    1 pound natural Swiss cheese, shredded
    2 cups Sauvignon Blanc
    2 tablespoons brandy
    1 clove garlic
    Nutmeg

Coat cheese with flour by shaking together in a paper bag. Heat wine until nearly boiling. Reduce heat, slowly adding mixture of flour and cheese. Stir constantly with wooden spoon until smooth and creamy. Add brandy and stir. Add a few pinches of nutmeg at the last.

Rub interior of fondue pot generously with garlic clove. Pour in cheese mixture, and serve hot with cubed French bread or raw vegetables.

For flavor and consistency, unprocessed cheese such as Gruyere or Emmanthaler is suggested.

Try with: Sauvignon Blanc

BRIE EN CROUTE WITH PESTO

Buena Vista Winery
Elaine Bell

This was created for the KQED Wine & Food Festival, and is sufficient for a large group.

2½ pounds puff pastry dough, fresh, or frozen and thawed
1 egg, beaten
2 tablespoons pesto sauce
1 wheel (2½ pound) Brie, chilled

Roll the puff dough into a 12 by 24-inch rectangle. Cut the dough into two 10-inch rounds. Brush one round entirely with beaten egg. Spread 1 tablespoon pesto to cover all but a one-inch rim around the edge of the disc. Place the Brie on the pesto. Spread top of Brie with remaining pesto sauce. Place the second round over the Brie. Firmly press the top round to the bottom round to seal. Chill 30 minutes.

Brush with egg. With the point of a sharp knife, cut decorative slits in the dough. Bake in preheated 400° oven for 40 to 50 minutes. Serve at once.

Italian Pesto
A Standard Version

½ cup fresh basil leaves, very finely chopped
6 cloves garlic, finely minced
¼ cup parsley, finely chopped
½ cup olive oil
6 tablespoons parmesan cheese, grated

To make about a cup, blend the above until it becomes a paste, adding a small amount of boiling water if necessary. A food processor is ideal for pesto, but it may be made by other means. Pesto may be frozen as a garnish for soups, pasta, meats, etc.

CUCUMBER-CHIVE CANAPES   **Buena Vista Winery**
Elaine Bell, for KQED Wine & Food Festival

2 cucumbers, peeled and seeded
½ bunch chives, finely chopped
1 pound cream cheese, softened
  Salt to taste

Reserve a bit of chopped chives and tiny cucumber wedges for garnish. Purée cucumber and chives in a blender. Drain well. Combine well with cream cheese. Chill.

Spread on small toast rounds, garnished as above.

HORS d'OEUVRE LILA   **Adler Fels**

4 flour tortillas (from 18-ounce package)
1 package (3-ounce) smoked sliced salmon, cut in pieces
1 yellow onion, finely chopped
1 package (8-ounce) cream cheese, softened
1 jar caviar (2-ounce, any inexpensive kind)
  Butter, softened
  Foil

Place one tortilla on a double thickness of foil. Spread cream cheese on tortilla. Spread chopped onions on cream cheese. Place another tortilla on top and press down with a spatula. Spread cream cheese on this second tortilla and place salmon pieces evenly on top. Add another tortilla, press down, spread cream cheese and caviar on top. Add the last tortilla and press down. Spread butter on top and place in preheated 350° oven. Press down occasionally to keep the top tortilla from turning up. Bake until golden brown and crisp. Remove from oven and let cool five minutes. Cut in one- or two-inch pieces and serve hot.

If you wish, use very large tortillas and double the filling.

Try with: Fumé Blanc

PATÉ MAISON JILL   **Sterling Vineyards**

¼ cup butter
1 pound chicken livers
1 cup white wine
1 clove garlic, chopped
1 medium onion, minced
½ teaspoon dried basil

Sauté garlic and onion in melted butter until onion is clear. Add livers, turning frequently until browned. Add wine and basil and cook ten minutes, stirring occasionally. Let cool. Blend in food processor or blender until smooth and creamy. Pour into lightly greased mold and chill.

Try with: Sauvignon Blanc, Chardonnay

SPRING CHICKEN SLICES   **Sterling Vineyards**

3 whole chicken breasts, split and boned
½ cup red wine
¼ cup soy sauce
½ teaspoon sugar
   Garlic salt to taste
¼ cup unflavored cooking oil

Mix marinade ingredients and marinate chicken breasts at least 24 hours. Broil breasts for five minutes (or less) on each side. Return to marinade. Slice meat very thinly and serve on thin crackers, or in larger portions with a garnish of fresh fruit. This preparation will keep, refrigerated, for up to two weeks.

SALMON PATÉ   Hanns Kornell Champagne Cellars

   1 pound raw fillet of sole, chopped very fine by hand
   1 cup butter
   1 cup fresh bread crumbs
  ¼ cup heavy cream
   2 egg yolks, beaten
  ½ cup parsley, chopped
  ½ cup shallots, chopped
  ½ cup dill weed, chopped
     Salt, cayenne pepper to taste.
1½ to 2 pounds salmon steaks, thinly sliced, boned, and
     skinned
     Mace
  ¼ cup butter

Mix together sole and 1 cup butter. Soak crumbs in cream.

Combine sole mixture, crumbs, cream and spices with yolks and mix until light and fluffy.

Line loaf-size terrine or baking dish with one-half inch of sole mixture (forcemeat) and cover with salmon steaks. Layer forcemeat and salmon until dish is full, seasoning steaks with salt and mace as you go. Dot top with ¼ cup butter. Cover terrine tightly (with foil if no other cover is available).

Bake at 300° (slow oven) for 2½ hours. Let cool before removing cover. Unmold on watercress or green leaf lettuce. Coat with green mayonnaise.

Try with: Champagne

Green Mayonnaise

Combine one part dairy sour cream to two parts mayonnaise. Blend in to taste: parsley, green onions, and watercress, all finely minced.

ROLLED ITALIAN CHICKEN   Cakebread Cellars
To prepare a day before serving

     1 chicken, 2½ pounds, completely boned
        Salt and pepper to taste
     ¼ pound baked ham, thinly sliced
     ⅓ cup toasted bread crumbs
     1 teaspoon oregano
     ¼ cup parsley, minced
    10 soft, oil-cured black olives, pitted and sliced
     ¼ pound salami, very thinly sliced
     3 hard-cooked eggs
        Oregano to taste
        Bacon strips

Bone the chicken, or have butcher do this for you. Reserve wings, neck, giblets, and bones for stock.

Spread chicken skin-side down on sheet of waxed paper. Fold meat in from the legs, forming meat in as even a layer as possible. Sprinkle chicken with salt and pepper to taste. Cover meat with waxed paper and pound to uniform thickness.

Remove waxed paper. Cover chicken with ham slices. In small bowl, combine bread crumbs, parsley, oregano and pepper to taste. Sprinkle ham layer with half of this mixture and place sliced olives on top to form another layer.

Arrange salami over olives. Arrange eggs lengthwise down center of chicken. Fold in the ends of chicken and, beginning at one of the long sides, roll meat tightly around eggs. Tie this with kitchen string at one-inch intervals, making sure that chicken skin encloses all the filling.

Sprinkle this roll with oregano, salt and pepper to taste, and place in roasting pan seam-side down. Cover top with bacon strips. Roast at 350° for 50 minutes, basting several times with drippings.

Discard bacon. Increase heat to 425°. Bake for 10 or 15 more minutes, or until lightly brown. Let roll cool completely, and chill overnight.

Slice the roll, arrange slices on platter, and let stand at room temperature for one hour before serving.

Serves 6 to 8

Try with: Cabernet Sauvignon

Soups

CREAM OF SPINACH SOUP

Domaine Chandon
Philippe Jeanty

    2 pounds fresh spinach, washed and drained
       Chicken stock or water sufficient to boil spinach
    4 tablespoons sweet butter (½ stick)
    2 cups heavy cream

Bring water or stock to boil, add the spinach and cook until tender.

Drain off most of the liquid, reserving some to adjust soup thickness later if necessary.

Blend or purée cooked spinach and pass through a fine sieve. The soup should be neither too watery, nor too thick. Thin with reserved cooking liquid if necessary.

Remove from heat, add cream, butter (cut in pieces) and salt to taste. Serve hot.

Serves 10 or 12

AVOCADO SOUP   Robert Mondavi Winery

- 2 medium carrots, finely diced
- 1 large onion, finely diced
- 2 stalks celery, finely diced
- 2 tablespoons butter
- 4 (13-ounce) cans chicken broth, or an equal amount of homemade broth
- 3 whole garlic cloves
- 3 stalks parsley
- 2 large ripe avocados, peeled and diced into half-inch cubes
- 3 tablespoons sherry

Sauté carrots, onion and celery in butter over medium heat until limp. Add chicken broth, garlic and parsley; bring to boil. Reduce heat and simmer for 30 minutes. Remove garlic and parsley. Add avocado and cook until just heated. Stir in sherry. Serve in mugs.

Serves 6 to 8

Try with: Fumé Blanc

"Serve in earthenware mugs, accompanied by toast rounds topped with small strips of marinated salmon and capers."

APPLE-ONION SOUP   Hanns Kornell Champagne Cellars

2 green apples, peeled, cored and sliced
1 Bermuda onion, sliced
2 tablespoons melted butter
3 cans beef consommé
1 teaspoon curry powder (approximately, to taste)
½ cup half & half or whole milk

Sauté apples and onions in butter until onions are transparent, stirring in the curry powder at this time. Add consommé and bring to a simmer. Cover and simmer 25 minutes. Remove from heat.

Fill blender one-third full and purée. Repeat until entire mixture is blended. Return to pan, add the half & half, and heat slowly.

Serves 4

GINGER SQUASH SOUP   Chateau St. Jean
Linda Hagen

2 tablespoons butter
1 onion, sliced
1 garlic clove
1 acorn or butternut squash, peeled and cubed to
    half-inch pieces
2 cups chicken broth
6 slices ginger
1 cup heavy cream
2 tablespoons dry sherry
1 tablespoon lime juice

Sauté onion until transparent. Add garlic, ginger, squash and broth. Simmer until squash is tender (approximately 20 minutes). Purée, in food processor if available. Add cream, sherry and lime juice.

Serves 4

Try with: Johannisberg Riesling, Gewurztraminer

THE FARMER'S VEGETABLE SOUP   Winery Lake

The following recipe was suggested by Veronica di Rosa, illustrator of "Entertaining in the Light Style", by Lou Seibert Pappas, and wife of Rene di Rosa, a pioneer grower in the Carneros area, which until very recently was included in the Napa Valley, and now has an appellation of its own. Mrs. Pappas recommends this soup with French bread and an assortment of cheeses as the nourishing base of a blind wine-tasting party — one variety of wine in several different styles, disguised in numbered brown paper bags until judgment has been passed.

2 tablespoons butter
1 large onion, finely chopped
2 bunches leeks, sliced
2 quarts rich chicken stock
3 medium potatoes
2 teaspoons fresh tarragon, chopped (or ½ teaspoon
    dried tarragon, crumbled)
  Salt and freshly ground black pepper, to taste
¼ cup parsley, finely chopped
2 cups (1 pint) whipping cream
4 ounces Gruyere or Fontina cheese, grated

In large saucepan, melt butter and sauté onion and leeks until glazed. Add stock, potatoes, tarragon, salt and pepper. Cover and simmer for 15 minutes, or until tender. Purée in a food processor or mash with a potato masher. Ladle into soup bowls and sprinkle with parsley.

Pass a pitcher of cream and a bowl of grated cheese for guests to add as desired.

Serves 8

Try with: Zinfandel, Cabernet Sauvignon, Sauvignon Blanc, Chenin Blanc

PRESTEN'S SPLIT PEA SOUP   **Sterling Vineyards**

        1 or 2 ham hocks
    ½ pound bacon, finely cut
        2 large onions, chopped
        3 large carrots, thinly sliced
        2 large potatoes, diced
        1 cup green split peas, uncooked
        4 cups water
        2 cups Chardonnay
        1 can beef consommé (10½ ounces, undiluted)
        1 bay leaf
        1 tablespoon Worcestershire sauce
        1 tablespoon soy sauce
    ½ teaspoon black pepper, coarsely ground
            Salt to taste
            Vinegar

In a large kettle with cover, sauté bacon until cooked but not crisp. Add onions and sauté until limp. Add remaining ingredients, except salt and vinegar. Cover and simmer 2 hours, stirring often.

Mash with potato masher until smooth (or remove bacon bits, press through a coarse sieve, and return bits to soup later, or whirl in blender until smooth).

Reheat and correct seasoning with salt, pepper, Worcestershire sauce, and vinegar, if desired.

Serves 6 to 8

Try with: Chardonnay, Merlot

RED BELL PEPPER SOUP   **Beringer Vineyards**
California Culinary Academy Scholarship Winner

- 2 tablespoons olive oil
- 2 pounds red bell peppers (approximately 10-12 medium). Green bell peppers may be substituted, but they will not have the natural sweetness of the red.
- 1 onion, chopped
- 4 cloves garlic, chopped
- 4 cups chicken stock
- 2 teaspoons coriander, minced
- 6 tablespoons sour cream

Clean, de-seed and chop peppers. Sauté onions, garlic and peppers in olive oil until tender (approximately 10 minutes), shaking pan occasionally to prevent burning. Add half the chicken stock and cook for ten more minutes.

At this point, either remove from heat to strain the mixture for a creamier texture, or leave as is for a chunkier-style soup.

Add the rest of the chicken stock and simmer until the desired consistency is reached. Season with coriander. For richer flavor, stir in cream. Remove from heat. Garnish each serving with 1 tablespoon sour cream. Serve hot or cold.

Serves 6

Try with: Fumé Blanc, Sauvignon Blanc

Main Courses

Fish & Seafood

BAKED SALMON WITH WINE Charles Krug Winery

1 six-pound tail section of salmon, seasoned with salt and
    pepper
1 carrot, finely chopped
1 onion, finely chopped
2 stalks celery, finely chopped
4 tablespoons butter
    Dash of dried thyme
2 bay leaves
5 sprigs parsley
4 cups Fumé Blanc or Chablis

Sauté vegetables until golden in a pan with a cover that will
tolerate your oven and is large enough for the salmon. Place
fish on vegetables in pan and add herbs and wine.

Cover fish with buttered waxed paper or aluminum foil and
bring wine to a boil on top of stove.

Cover pan and place in hot oven (425°) for about an hour, or
until fish flakes easily, basting fish from time to time.

Place fish on warm serving dish, fillet it with a wide spatula
— the meat should lift off easily — and remove skin.

Strain the pan liquid into saucepan and cook briskly until
reduced to half. Cream 1½ tablespoons flour with 3
tablespoons butter and stir into pan liquid until sauce is
thickened. Add salt and freshly-ground pepper.

Pour sauce over fish or serve on the side. Garnish serving dish
with sliced red peppers and mushrooms.

Serves 10 to 12

Try with: Fumé Blanc, Chardonnay

FISH MOUSSE with SHRIMP SAUCE   Trefethen Vineyards

Make this any time — it freezes well.

Mousse:

1½ pounds shrimp in the shell, uncooked
½ pound sea scallops
2 shallots, medium size
1¼ teaspoon salt and white pepper
½ teaspoon Tabasco sauce
½ teaspoon nutmeg, freshly grated (scant measure)
2 egg whites
2 cups heavy cream

Peel and devein shrimp. Reserve shells for sauce (below). Rinse, drain and dry scallops.

Depending on capacity of food processor, you may find it necessary to process in two batches.

Fit work bowl of food processor with steel blade. Turn machine on and drop shallots through feed tube until finely minced. Turn machine off, add shrimp and a little egg white. Process until very smooth, about 90 seconds. Scrape down sides occasionally.

Add scallops and slowly add egg white. Blend until smooth. Add salt, Tabasco, and nutmeg, and process until well mixed, scraping down sides. With machine running, gradually add cream. Mix until well blended and mixture is thickened.

If you do not plan to use this mixture immediately, cover and refrigerate for up to 24 hours.

Pour into *well-greased* 5- to 6-cup ring mold, or individual molds. Smooth top with spatula. Cover with waxed paper and aluminum foil. Place in *bain marie* and bake 25 to 45 minutes to interval temperature of 155 to 165°.

Let firm up for 5 minutes. Unmold and spoon shrimp sauce around base. Garnish with shrimp.

NOTE: *In place of the shrimp and scallops, you may use ⅓ sole, ⅓ snapper, and ⅓ ling cod.*

Shrimp Sauce

    1 to 1¼ pounds small whole shrimp
1½ cups full-bodied fish stock
    2 tablespoons shallots, finely minced
    2 tablespoons butter
1½ cups Creme Fraiche or heavy cream
    ¼ cup Vermouth
      Beurre manie
      Chives, chervil, or parsley, finely minced
    4 to 6 tablespoons butter, to enrich sauce if necessary

In heavy saucepan melt the 2 tablespoons butter, and add shallots and fish stock with some vermouth. Bring to boil, reduce heat, and add shrimp. Simmer until unpeeled shrimp just turn a bright pink.

Strain stock and return it to saucepan. Add vermouth and cook stock down until reduced by half. You should have about ¾ cup. While stock is cooking, peel shrimp and slice them in half lengthwise (if this seems too difficult, dice them instead) and set shrimp aside.

Add cream to reduced stock, bring to a boil, and again cook the mixture until reduced by half. Whisk in bits of beurre manie just enough to thicken the sauce slightly. Whisk in butter and correct seasoning.

Return shrimp to sauce and gently heat through.

NOTE: *This sauce must not boil. In place of the shrimp, one pound of tiny bay scallops may be substituted.*

Try with: Chardonnay

SALMON MOUSSE   Heitz Wine Cellars
To prepare one day before serving

> 2 envelopes unflavored gelatin
> ½ cup water
> 2 tablespoons white wine
> 2 tablespoons vinegar
> 2 tablespoons lemon juice
> 1 teaspoon horseradish
>   Dash freshly ground pepper
> ½ cup mayonnaise
> ½ cup heavy cream, whipped, then mixed with mayonnaise
> 1½ pounds fresh-cooked salmon, or one 1-pound can salmon, drained
> 1 cup heavy cream, whipped

Remove skin and flake salmon finely.

Soften gelatin in water in top part of double boiler, stirring over heat until dissolved. Combine dissolved gelatin thoroughly with all ingredients except the last-mentioned cup of heavy cream.

Whip the remaining cream, and fold into above mixture.

Turn into lightly oiled mold large enough to hold 1½ quarts, or into lightly oiled individual serving molds. Cover with foil or plastic wrap and chill for at least 24 hours.

Unmold on a platter lined with lettuce leaves, or on individual plates. Garnish with the following Avocado Sauce, lemon wedges, cherry tomatoes, and watercress.

Serves 8

Try with: Chardonnay

Avocado Sauce

    3 ripe avocados
    ½ cup heavy cream, whipped
    1 teaspoon lemon or lime juice
      Dash cayenne pepper

Whip cream and set aside. Pit and peel avocados and puree in food processor (or blender, or mash with wooden spoon in bowl). Add citrus juice and cayenne. Fold in whipped cream. Serve a small amount on each individual portion.

HUITRES AU CHAMPAGNE   **Domaine Chandon**
                                  Philippe Jeanty

    12 fresh oysters, with juice reserved
     1 shallot, minced
     1 cup heavy cream
     ½ cup Blanc de Noirs (dry sparkling wine)
     1 tablespoon sweet butter
     2 tablespoons watercress, finely chopped (optional)

Shuck oysters, being careful to reserve juice. Scrub shells to serve in later.

Place oysters in saucepan with their juice. Cook for 2 or 3 minutes. Remove oysters and keep them warm.

Add cream, wine, and minced shallot to the hot oyster juice and stir until sauce is reduced in volume by one-third. Swirl in butter and add watercress, if desired. Taste and correct seasoning if necessary.

Serve oysters in their shells with a bit of sauce in each one. Garnish with julienned vegetables if desired.

Serves 2 as a first course.

Try with: Napa Valley Brut, dry sparkling wine

MARINATED SCALLOP SALAD   Robert Mondavi Winery

 1 pound scallops (cut in half if large)
 3 tablespoons lime juice
 5 tablespoons lemon juice
 1 small red onion
 1 large ripe avocado, peeled
 3 tablespoons white wine or Fumé Blanc
 ½ cup olive oil
 ¼ teaspoon orange zest
 1 teaspoon orange juice
 ½ teaspoon Dijon mustard
   Salt and pepper
   Boston lettuce leaves
   Orange sections, peeled, with membranes removed

Marinate scallops in lime juice and 3 tablespoons of the lemon juice for two hours. Drain.

Combine a dressing of olive oil, remaining lemon juice, wine, orange zest and juice, and mustard.

Thinly slice scallops (about ¼ inch thick). Thinly slice onion and separate into rings. Dice avocado into ¾ inch cubes.

Gently toss scallops, onion and avocado with dressing and arrange on individual plates (or a large shallow bowl for transporting) lined with "cups" of lettuce leaves. Lightly sprinkle with salt and pepper and garnish with orange sections.

Serves 4 on a picnic, or 6 as a first course at dinner

Try with: Fumé Blanc

CRAB RIESLING   Scottie McKinney

    3 pounds fresh crab meat
    ½ cup green onions, chopped
    2 bunches watercress, cleaned and chopped
    ½ cup olive oil
    ½ cup dry Riesling
    ¼ cup pistachio nuts
    2 teaspoons dry mustard
    ¼ teaspoon salt

Combine in food processor or blender: olive oil, wine, nuts, mustard, and salt. Blend until smooth. Toss with crab and green onions. Serve on bed of chopped watercress.

Serves 4 to 6

Try with: Dry Riesling

SEA BASS SAUVIGNON   Whitehall Lane

    1 to 1½ pounds fillets of sea bass (or any firm white fish)
    ½ cup flour
    1½ sticks sweet butter
    1¼ cups Sauvignon Blanc
    1 tablespoon shallots, chopped
    1 clove garlic, finely chopped
    ¼ cup cream
    ½ teaspoon seasoning salt
    ½ teaspoon sugar
    1 shake cayenne pepper
      Chives, finely chopped

Dredge fish in flour, shake off excess, and sauté lightly in butter. Transfer to warmed plate and keep warm.

Deglaze skillet with wine, add shallots and garlic, and cook until reduced to half. Add cream, salt, sugar, and cayenne. Simmer for 5 minutes over low heat, stirring often.

Pour sauce over fish, top with chives and serve immediately.

Serves 4 to 6

Try with: Sauvignon Blanc

GOLDEN COQUILLES ST. JACQUES   **Louis M. Martini**

2 cups Chardonnay or other dry white wine
1 cup water
1 cup yellow onion, carrot, and celery, sliced and mixed
1 bay leaf
4 whole allspice
6 whole peppercorns
1½ pounds fresh scallops, medium to large
   Salt, freshly ground white pepper
1 cup sour cream
   Fresh lemon juice
4 ounces Golden Caviar
¼ cup green onion, chopped
6 to 8 lemon wedges

In a small, heavy saucepan bring wine, water, vegetables, bay leaf and peppercorns to boil and simmer 20 minutes over low heat. Meanwhile, pat scallops dry and season lightly with salt and pepper.

Strain the mixture, return to pan, bring to boil, and add the scallops very briefly, turning them once or twice until mixture just barely comes to another boil. Remove immediately. Do not overcook scallops! If desired, cut scallops into smaller pieces. Set aside to cool.

Stir sour cream until smooth and creamy. Add a little lemon juice. Toss scallops in sour cream until well coated.

Top each serving with a tablespoon of caviar and garnish with chopped green onion and a lemon wedge.

Serves 6

Try with: Chardonnay

SOLE CALEDONIA   **Flora Springs**

     1 pound fillet of sole
    ½ cup dry white wine
     1 cup asparagus, cut in pieces
    ½ cup to 1 cup fresh mushrooms, sliced
    ½ cup cherry tomato halves
     2 tablespoons butter or margarine
     2 tablespoons flour
    ½ teaspoon salt
       Dash white pepper
    1¼ cups milk
     1 egg yolk, slightly beaten
    ¼ cup dry white wine
     1 cup soft bread crumbs
    ¼ cup grated Parmesan cheese

In covered medium-sized skillet poach fish in ½ cup wine for about three minutes, or until fish flakes easily with fork. Drain and arrange in lightly greased baking dish (suggested size: 10x6x2 inches). Season lightly with salt. Top with asparagus, tomatoes, and mushrooms.

Melt butter over low heat in small saucepan and stir in flour, salt and pepper. Add milk, stirring constantly until mixture thickens and bubbles. Stir a small amount of this hot mixture into the egg yolk, to prevent curdling, and return to saucepan, stirring until mixture returns to a boil. Remove from heat, stir in remaining wine, and pour evenly over fillets and vegetables in baking dish.

Sprinkle bread crumbs combined with parmesan cheese over all. Bake uncovered in 350° oven for 30 minutes.

Serves 4

Try with: Sauvignon Blanc

SEAFOOD GUMBO   Matanzas Creek Winery

Stock

> 3 quarts water
> Shrimp shells and/or top shells (only) of crabs (see
>   below)
> 3 carrots
> 3 stalks celery
> 2 onions, quartered
> 2 bay leaves
> Parsley (several sprigs)

Simmer above ingredients over slow heat until boiled down to
2 quarts. Strain and set aside.

Gumbo

> 2 to 3 cups peeled shrimp (prawns), shells reserved for
>   stock
> 1 California Dungeness crab or 3 Gulf of Mexico crabs,
>   broken into eighths or quarters, respectively, top
>   shells reserved for stock
> 2 to 3 cups raw shelled oysters
> ½ stick butter
> 1 large onion, chopped
> 2 cups green onion, chopped
> 2 cups okra, sliced
> 1 16-ounce can whole tomatoes
> 1 cup green peppers, finely chopped
> 3 tablespoons butter
> 3 tablespoons flour
> 2 quarts Stock (above)
> 1 tablespoon gumbo filé powder (optional)
> Salt, pepper, cayenne to taste
> 3 cups cooked rice

Melt the half-stick butter in large pot and sauté onion, green onion, okra, and green peppers.

In separate large frying pan make a roux of the 3 tablespoons butter and flour, cooking slowly and stirring constantly until brown. Add tomatoes and filé powder and cook to a paste. Add some stock to the roux, then add roux to sautéed mixture, followed by remaining stock. Bring to a simmer and add crab, shrimp, and oysters. Add salt, pepper, and cayenne to taste (should be good and spicy). Simmer 1½ hours. Serve in large soup bowls over rice.

Serves 6, generously.

Try with: Cabernet

Shallots

Meat

LAMB BARBECUE MARINADE   Frog's Leap Winery

- 1 handful fresh rosemary
- 1 bunch cilantro (coriander), stems removed
- 1 cup red wine
- 1 small jar Dijon mustard
- 2 tablespoons olive oil
- 2 sips brandy (about a jigger)
- 2 tablespoons soy sauce
- 1 tablespoon freshly ground pepper
- 2 large heads garlic, broken apart, but peeling unnecessary
- 2 jalapeno peppers (optional)

Mix all ingredients in food processor. Trim fat from meat and marinate overnight in the resulting marinade.

The above marinade is excellent for any cut of lamb.

For 8 lamb chops, two inches thick, barbecue lamb over hot fire, covered, for five minutes on each side. Add a handful of fresh rosemary to the fire when you turn the meat.

Try with: Zinfandel

ST. HELENA ROAST LAMB   Beringer Vineyards
California Culinary Academy Scholarship Winner

> 2 boned loins of lamb
> Caul fat, usually purchased separately from butcher
> Rosemary
> Fennel root, coarsely chopped
> 1 cup Cabernet Sauvignon
> Chanterelle, Oyster, and Shitake mushrooms, finely chopped
> Butter

Wrap boned loin of lamb around chopped fennel root and sprig of rosemary. Wrap whole loin in caul fat.

Sear the roast at 450° for 20 minutes.

Prepare sauce of 2 cups demi-glace, flavored with a bit of rosemary. Reduce the wine to one tablespoon by boiling rapidly; add to the demi-glace. Reduce this mixture further until it clings to the back of a spoon.

Garnish with the chopped mushrooms sautéed in butter.

Serves 6

Try with: Cabernet Sauvignon

NOTE: Demi-glace is rather complicated and time-consuming to make. Food editors polled said, "It definitely won't be the same thing, but a substitute could be any brown sauce or gravy," recipes for which may be found in most standard cookbooks.

MARINATED SWEETBREAD SALAD
Robert Mondavi Winery

  1½ pounds sweetbreads
  3 tablespoons butter
  6 shallots
  1 cucumber, peeled, seeded, and cut into ¼-inch slices
  ¼ cup Fumé Blanc
    Lemon dressing (recipe below)
    Orange zest (recipe below)
    Romaine lettuce

Devein sweetbreads and cut into small slices approximately ¾-inch square by ¼-inch thick. Heat butter in small skillet. When butter is very hot, add portion of sweetbread slices, and cook about a minute, turning, until just cooked through. Remove to bowl and repeat cooking cycle with remaining slices.

Slice shallots ¼-inch thick, separate into rings and place in ¼ cup of wine. Set aside. Meanwhile, make Lemon Dressing and Orange Zest. When these are completed, drain liquid from shallots to use in Lemon Dressing.

Toss cucumber slices, sweetbreads and drained shallots in dressing and allow to marinate for five minutes.

Arrange sweetbread mixture on bed of lettuce on individual serving dishes. Lightly scatter orange zest over top.

Try with: Fumé Blanc

Lemon Dressing

Combine ½ cup olive oil, ¼ cup salad oil, ¼ cup lemon juice, ½ teaspoon Dijon mustard, juice of ½ an orange, salt, and freshly ground black pepper to taste. Stir in the wine in which the shallots marinated.

Orange Zest

Gently pare thin layers of rind of one orange in long slices, taking only the orange zest and none of the white part. Place zest in small saucepan with ¼ cup water and 1 teaspoon sugar. Cook over high heat and boil until water evaporates, leaving zest dry at bottom of pan. Remove immediately so that zest does not burn.

SAGE ZINFANDEL PORK CHOPS
Shirley Sarvis
Cakebread Cellars

Pork must be cooked only to just-doneness in order to be properly juicy. Garnish with fresh sage leaves, if possible.

4 center-cut loin pork chops, about ½ pound each and trimmed of excess fat, cut 1¼ inches thick, and near room temperature when prepared
Salt
Freshly ground black pepper
6 tablespoons minced fresh sage leaves (or dried sage to season)
About 1 tablespoon light olive oil, or tried-out pork fat
¼ cup Zinfandel

Season surfaces of each chop generously with salt and pepper, and press in sage. Let stand for 30 minutes.

Heat a small amount of oil in a large, heavy frying pan over medium-high heat. Add chops and brown lightly on one side, turn, reduce heat to medium or low, and cook, turning occasionally, until juices run almost clear (rather than pink) when tested with a small slash near bone — about 8 to 10 minutes total.

Add wine to pan and cook, stirring, to loosen pan drippings and reduce to a thin glaze. Spoon over chops.

Serves 4

Try with: Zinfandel

DOLMAS

Richard Alexei
Monticello Cellars

Can be made in advance and refrigerated until ready to serve warm or cold.

Filling

   1 medium onion, finely chopped
   ¼ cup olive oil
   ¾ pound very lean ground lamb
   ½ cup white rice
   ½ cup white wine
   1 tablespoon tomato paste
   1 tablespoon dried dill weed or 3 tablespoons fresh
   ¼ cup pine nuts (or walnuts)
   1 teaspoon salt
   Freshly ground black pepper

Heat olive oil in large, heavy skillet and sauté onion over medium heat until soft and translucent but not brown. Add ground lamb and sauté a few minutes more until meat turns a rosy gray. Stir while cooking to blend meat and onions together thoroughly. Add remaining ingredients and stir to blend. Bring to boil over high heat, then cover and simmer over low heat for 10 to 15 minutes until liquid is absorbed and rice swells. Rice should be softened, but not completely cooked. Remove from heat and reserve.

Stuff grape leaves with above mixture, as follows:

   1 jar grape leaves (about 35 leaves)
   Beef broth
   ⅓ cup olive oil
   Juice of 1 lemon
   Waxed paper or cooking parchment
   Garnish of fresh chopped dill weed and lemon slices

Rinse grape leaves under cold running water and separate carefully. Place a leaf smooth-side down on the table and put about 1 tablespoon filling on the wide half. The exact amount of filling will vary according to the size and formation of the grape leaf. The filling should not spill out as you roll up the leaf, but don't be stingy, either. After you've done a few, you'll know just how much filling to use.

Bring up the wide sections of the leaf, then fold in the sides, and roll up to form a compact cylinder not too tightly, as the rice will swell as it cooks. With practice, you will pick up assembly speed to the point that you can roll up a batch in 10 minutes or less.

Arrange the stuffed leaves in one or two layers in a large pot or skillet. Add beef broth to half-way up the pot, then add olive oil and lemon juice.

Cut waxed paper or parchment to the size of the pot and place on top of the stuffed leaves (*dolmathes*). Cover tightly. Bring to a boil, then lower heat to maintain a slow simmer for 30 or 40 minutes. Liquid should be reduced to a glaze — if not, continue simmering uncovered to reduce it.

Remove *dolmathes* to a bowl or platter and pour the reduced cooking liquid or glaze over them.

Garnish with fresh chopped dill and lemon slices.

CARRIE'S BRATWURST SUPREME   **Flora Springs**

> 6 Bratwurst (veal sausage), 6-ounce size, sliced into ¼ inch slices
> 1 pound asparagus, cleaned and cut into one-inch pieces
> ¼ pound mushrooms, stemmed and sliced
> ¾ cup Sauvignon Blanc (or more, to taste)
> ¼ cup olive oil

Use large (12-inch) skillet with cover. Sauté sausage in olive oil and add asparagus and mushrooms. Stir together, add wine, cover, and cook 8 to 10 minutes. Serve with an egg dish such as soufflé or omelet and sourdough French bread.

Serves 4 to 6

Try with: Sauvignon Blanc

VEAL ELIZABETTA   Sebastiani Vineyards

  4 tablespoons butter
  4 tablespoons olive oil
    Flour
 12 thin slices veal scallopini
  2 cloves garlic, minced or mashed
  4 anchovy fillets
  2 dozen pitted Italian olives
  4 whole, peeled canned tomatoes
  4 leaves fresh basil or 1 teaspoon dried basil
  1 sprig parsley, chopped
    Salt and pepper to taste
  2 tablespoons capers
  ½ cup Cabernet Sauvignon

Heat butter and oil in large, heavy skillet. Pass veal through flour and shake off excess. Sauté meat for 1 minute on each side. Set aside.

Sauté garlic, anchovies and olives for one or two minutes, mashing anchovies with fork. Add tomatoes, basil, and parsley and heat to boiling, breaking up tomatoes with a fork. Reduce heat.

Add salt, pepper, capers, wine and meat and simmer on low heat for 5 minutes.

Serves 4

Try with: Cabernet Sauvignon

Poultry

CHICKEN DIJON IN PHYLLO

Chateau St. Jean
Linda Hagen

1 package phyllo leaves (20 sheets)
5 chicken breasts, deboned and cubed
5 large mushrooms, chopped
4 tablespoons shallots, minced
5 tablespoons green onions, chopped
½ stick butter
¼ cup Dijon mustard
1 to 2 cups whipping cream
½ cup dry white wine
½ teaspoon tarragon
    Salt, white pepper
1 tablespoon flour
    Crumbs from 5 slices bread, toasted
1 stick butter, melted

Sauté chicken in salt, pepper and butter for five minutes, or until no longer pink. Remove from pan. Sauté shallots, green onions, and mushrooms. Add flour, wine, mustard, cream and tarragon. Adjust seasoning to taste. Remove from heat. Return chicken to pan and let cool.

Fold one sheet phyllo and brush with melted butter. Sprinkle with crumbs. Top with another buttered sheet of phyllo. Spread chicken mixture on top of this, and roll up. Brush with butter. Bake at 450° for 15 minutes.

Serves 10

Try with: Chardonnay, Fumé Blanc

BRANDY-BUTTERED ROAST TURKEY

The Christian Brothers

    1 turkey, 12 to 14 pounds, ready to cook
      Salt
      Pepper
    ½ cup olive oil
    ½ cup butter
    ½ cup brandy

Rub body and neck cavities of turkey lightly with salt and pepper.

Fill cavities loosely with stuffing per recipe below. If preferred, stuffing can be baked in a covered casserole during the last hour the turkey roasts.

Skewer openings, tie legs close to body, and turn wing tips back under body. Place on rack in shallow roasting pan. Brush skin with oil. Roast in moderately slow oven (325°) until skin begins to color (about 1½ hours).

Melt butter with brandy. Baste turkey with brandy-butter about every 20 minutes, continuing to roast about 2 to 2½ hours longer, until drumstick can be moved up and down easily and fleshy part of drumstick feels soft and tender when pressed with fingers protected with folded paper towel.

Brother Timothy's Turkey Stuffing

    1 12-ounce package frozen chopped spinach, thawed
    1 pound pork sausage meat
    ¼ pound chicken or turkey livers
    1 cup sausage drippings and butter
    1 cup chopped onion
    ½ teaspoon rosemary, crumbled
    ½ teaspoon mint flakes
      One-eighth teaspoon nutmeg
    ½ cup chicken broth, or ½ cup water and 1 chicken
      bouillon cube
    ½ cup brandy
    1 teaspoon salt
      One-eighth teaspoon pepper
    3 quarts soft day-old bread crumbs
    ½ cup toasted blanched almonds
    ⅓ cup grated Parmesan cheese

Drain spinach well, pressing out excess moisture. Brown sausage. Cut livers in small pieces and add to skillet when sausage is about half cooked. Scoop out meats and set aside. Measure drippings and add butter to make 1 cup. Add onion, rosemary, mint flakes, and nutmeg. Cook slowly until onion is soft but not browned. Add broth, brandy, salt, pepper and spinach. Heat to simmering. Pour over bread to moisten easily. Stir in almonds and cheese. Makes about 2⅓ quarts.

Stuff bird before roasting, or bake in covered casserole in moderately slow oven for about an hour.

Serves 8 to 10

Try with: Zinfandel, Gamay Noir, Napa Rosé, Chardonnay, Chenin Blanc

BUBBEH CHICKEN   Whitehall Lane Winery

1 roasting chicken, as large as possible
3 carrots, chopped
2 celery stalks, chopped
2 onions, chopped
3 cloves garlic, chopped
  Seasoned salt
  Garlic powder
  Chicken stock
  Blanc de Pinot Noir

Toss vegetables together and place on bottom of roasting pan which has been sprayed with "Pam". Place chicken on bed of vegetables and sprinkle with seasonings. Place pan, uncovered, in a 450° oven for about half an hour, until chicken is nicely browned. Add equal parts of stock and wine to cover bottom of pan to a depth of ½ inch.

Cover pan and reduce oven heat to 325°. Baste chicken every 20 minutes with pan liquid. As liquid evaporates, replenish with wine. Cook for at least 1½ hours after covering pan.

Remove chicken to a warm platter and keep warm. Place pan juices and vegetables in a Pyrex cup, wait 5 minutes and skim off fat. Purée vegetables and liquid in blender and adjust seasonings.

Gently reheat sauce and serve with chicken over rice pilaf or melon seed pasta.

Try with: Blanc de Pinot Noir

CHICKEN BREASTS STUFFED WITH SHRIMP

Hanns Kornell Champagne Cellars

- 6 whole chicken breasts, halved, skinned and boned
- 6 tablespoons butter
- ½ pound mushrooms, thinly sliced
- ¾ cup green onions, thinly sliced
- 4 tablespoons flour
- ½ teaspoon thyme
- ¾ cup chicken stock
- ¾ cup dry champagne
- Milk
- Salt and pepper to taste
- 8 ounces crab meat
- 8 ounces small bay shrimp
- ½ cup dry breadcrumbs
- ½ cup chopped parsley
- 2 cups shredded Swiss cheese

Pound each half chicken breast between sheets of waxed paper until each is about ¼ inch thick.

Melt butter in frying pan over medium heat. Add mushrooms and onions and cook until onions are soft. Stir in flour and thyme and cook until mixture begins to bubble.

A little at a time, stir in chicken stock, champagne, and milk, stirring constantly until sauce thickens. Add salt and pepper and remove from heat.

In separate bowl, mix crab and shrimp with ½ cup of above sauce, bread crumbs and parsley. Spread this filling over each piece of chicken breast, and roll them up. Place the rolls, seam side down, in a buttered baking dish. Pour the remaining sauce over the chicken rolls and sprinkle with cheese.

Cover and bake at 400° for approximately 30 minutes, or until done.

Serves 6 to 12

Try with: Brut (dry Champagne)

CHICKEN FRONTIGNAN   **Beaulieu Vineyard**

4 pounds chicken, cut up, or 2½ pounds chicken breasts
　　or thighs
¼ cup flour, seasoned with salt and pepper
¼ cup olive oil
1 large onion, sliced thin
4 to 6 cloves garlic, sliced or minced
4 celery stalks, chopped
1 large carrot, coarsely chopped
1½ cups rich chicken broth (or use condensed, canned
　　chicken broth and cut down on salt in recipe)
3 ounces Muscat de Frontignan
1½ cups mushrooms, sliced and sautéed in butter
12 stuffed olives, sliced

Shake chicken pieces in paper bag with seasoned flour. Brown chicken in olive oil and put in large, buttered casserole that has a cover.

Sauté onion, garlic, celery and carrot for about 10 minutes in the same oil used for chicken. Meanwhile, add Muscat to broth and heat over high enough temperature to evaporate some of the alcohol. Add to casserole, cover, and bake for 1½ hours at 350°.

Just before serving, garnish with hot sautéed mushrooms and sliced olives.

Serves 6 generously.

Try with: Gamay Beaujolais

KIWI QUAIL   Scottie McKinney

 1 large ripe avocado, finely diced (about 1 cup)
 ½ cup fresh spinach leaves, chopped
 ½ cup walnuts, chopped
    Salt and freshly ground pepper to taste
 8 quail (or 4 Cornish game hens)
 ¼ cup melted butter
    Kiwi Sauce (recipe below)

Combine room temperature avocado, spinach, walnuts, salt and pepper. Stuff birds with this mixture and brush with melted butter. Grill over low mesquite fire for about ten minutes, turning each quail two or three times to brown evenly. (Adjust cooking time if game hens are used.) Serve with Kiwi Sauce.

Kiwi Sauce

 1 tablespoon shallots, chopped
 ¼ cup sweet butter
 6 kiwi fruits
 ½ teaspoon ground sage
 ½ teaspoon salt
 2 teaspoons honey
 ¾ cup dry Sauvignon Blanc

Sauté shallots in 1 tablespoon butter until soft, but not brown. Peel kiwi fruits. Combine shallot butter, kiwi, sage and salt —if using a food processor, quarter kiwi first and use steel blade — or chop kiwi finely before blending. Purée and place in top of double boiler with remaining butter and honey. Heat slowly, stirring constantly until sauce is hot and butter and honey are melted. Do not boil. Add wine and heat three to four minutes longer. Serve over quail or game hens.

Serves 4

Try with: Chardonnay, Cabernet Sauvignon

ROASTED CORNISH GAME HENS   **Louis M. Martini**

Stuffing [*for 6 Cornish game hens*]

  1 cup long grain white rice
  2 cups chicken stock
  ½ teaspoon salt
  1 tablespoon butter
  ¼ teaspoon ground cinnamon
  ¼ teaspoon ground cardamom
  1 teaspoon orange rind, freshly grated
  ½ cup chopped pitted dates
  ½ cup chopped pecans

Bring chicken stock, salt, butter, cinnamon, cardamom, and orange rind to a boil. Add rice, cover, and reduce heat. Simmer 20 minutes and let sit 5 minutes. Fluff with a fork and stir in dates and pecans.

Preheat oven to 350°.

Prepare the birds as follows:

  6 Cornish game hens
    Salt, pepper
  6 tablespoons butter, softened
  ½ cup orange marmalade
  ¼ cup Gewurtz Traminer

Rinse game hens and pat dry. Salt and pepper cavity and stuff with a generous ½ cup of rice mixture. Secure legs with kitchen string and place hens in a roasting pan. Brush hens with softened butter and roast for 30 minutes.

Melt orange marmalade with the wine and reduce slightly. Raise oven temperature to 400°, baste hens with marmalade mixture and continue roasting an additional 20 or 30 minutes, or until juices run clear and hens are browned. Baste occasionally with the marmalade mixture, and if the hens start to darken too much, cover with aluminum foil.

Serves 6

Try with: Gewurz Traminer

TURKEY KEBOBS   Gundlach-Bundschu Winery

Prepare 4 hours before broiling. Good served with barley pilaf.

Marinade

- ½ cup Late Harvest Riesling
- ¼ cup brown sugar
- ½ cup oil
- ⅔ cup soy sauce
- 1 teaspoon ground ginger or 1 tablespoon fresh ginger root, grated
- 1 clove garlic, minced
- 1 teaspoon lemon rind, grated
- 1 teaspoon paprika
- 4 green onions, minced
- 4 pounds turkey breast, skinned, boned, and cut into 2-inch cubes

Pour marinade over cubed turkey in shallow pan, and leave at room temperature for about four hours, stirring occasionally.

Prepare the following vegetables for skewering:

- 2 large zucchini, cut in ½-inch slices
- 8 to 12 cherry tomatoes
- 1 leek, sliced crosswise in ¼-inch pieces

In boiling salted water, cook the sliced leek for 2 minutes and the sliced zucchini for one minute. Drain. Run vegetables under cold water and pat dry.

Thread 8 10-inch skewers with the marinated turkey cubes, leek, zucchini, and cherry tomatoes. Arrange kebobs on rack of broiler pan and brush with marinade.

Broil about 4 inches from heat for four minutes, turn, baste again. Broil for another 4 to 5 minutes, or until turkey is firm.

Transfer to heated platter or individual plates. Sprinkle with parsley.

Serves 8

Try with: Johannisberg Riesling, Late Harvest Riesling

TURKEY SALAD

Inglenook Vineyards
Barbara Lang

Half a turkey breast (approximately 2¾ pounds)
3 tablespoons butter, softened
1 onion, sliced
¾ cup dry white wine
2 sprigs parsley
1 stalk celery, coarsely chopped
Dash of salt and pepper

Preheat oven to 350°. Place turkey breast on large piece of heavy foil. Smear the breast with butter. Fold sides of foil up and around meat and place remaining ingredients on top. Seal and crimp foil tightly, keeping it loose around the turkey. It is important that air circulate inside the foil, and also that no holes allow air or wine to escape.

Bake for 1¾ hours or until juice runs clear when turkey is pierced with a knife. Remove from oven and allow to cool while still wrapped in foil. When cool, remove breast from foil and discard other ingredients. Remove skin and separate meat from bone. Cut into cubes or julienne slices and set aside, covered.

Raspberry Vinaigrette

⅓ cup raspberry vinegar (if unavailable, see suggested
   substitute below)
1 cup olive oil
   Salt and pepper to taste
1 teaspoon orange peel, minced

Pour vinegar into large bowl and slowly whisk in oil. Add salt and pepper and toss in orange peel. Pour over the turkey and mix thoroughly.

Place turkey salad on plate and surround with alternating slices of orange and avocado. Garnish with mint leaves and raspberries.

Serves 4 as main course

Try with: Gamay Beaujolais

Barbara Lang suggests this substitute for Raspberry Vinegar when the real thing is not available: Mix together ¼ cup red wine vinegar, 2 tablespoons purée made from fresh or frozen raspberries, and ¾ teaspoon sugar.

PICNIC ROAST CHICKEN

Richard Alexei
Monticello Cellars

    1 3-pound broiler-fryer chicken
    2 cloves garlic
      Sprigs of fresh rosemary
      Olive oil
      Foil to wrap chicken in after cooking
      Salt and pepper to taste

Wash chicken and pat dry. Whack unpeeled garlic cloves with knife or cleaver to break slightly. Put garlic and rosemary into cavity of chicken and truss. Pat chicken dry with towel and rub a little olive oil into skin. Set on rack, breast up, in shallow pan. Roast in 475° oven for 15 to 20 minutes, or until chicken begins to brown. Lower heat to 350° and continue roasting for 45 to 60 minutes longer. Chicken should be slightly underdone, because when wrapped as described below it will cook further.

Immediately upon removing chicken from oven, wrap twice around in aluminum foil. Place in heavy brown paper grocery bag and close tightly. Chicken will stay warm for two hours. Carve to serve and season with salt and pepper to taste.

Serves 4 to 6.

Try with: Chardonnay, Sauvignon Blanc

POULARDE AUX MORILLES

Domaine Chandon
Philippe Jeanty

- 1 chicken, quartered
- 2 tablespoons butter
- 2 tablespoons oil
- 2 shallots, minced
- ⅔ cup Brut champagne or dry white wine
- 8 morels
- 1 cup heavy cream

Dried morels may be obtained at gourmet shops. Reconstitute the morels for one hour in a bowl of water, rinsing 5 or 6 times to remove all dirt. Clean out the "hairs" in the morels and blot them dry before using.

Sauté chicken in butter and oil for 10 minutes, or until brown. Add shallots and cook until soft but not brown. Deglaze the chicken and shallots with champagne or white wine, add the morels and cream and bring to a boil. Cook for about 2 minutes, then remove chicken and reduce sauce until thickened. Serve chicken napped with sauce.

Try with: Napa Valley Brut

SWEET-HOT CHICKEN

Valley of the Moon Winery

- 1 frying chicken, cut up
- 1 cup currant jelly
- 1 tablespoon horseradish
- 3 tablespoons prepared mustard
- ½ cup Ruby Port
- ½ cup orange juice
- ½ teaspoon powdered ginger
- 2 tablespoons butter
- 1 clove garlic, mashed
- ½ teaspoon Worcestershire sauce
  - Salt & pepper to taste

Simmer jelly, horseradish, mustard, Port, orange juice, ginger, butter, garlic and Worcestershire sauce together until butter and jelly melt. Season chicken with salt and pepper, and marinate in the sauce for 2 hours. Cover and bake at 350° for 45 minutes. Uncover, turn oven up to 400° and continue baking for 30 additional minutes. Serve with rice.

Serves 6

Meatless

HERB GOAT CHEESE SOUFFLÉ **Matanzas Creek Winery**

- 4 tablespoons butter
- 4 tablespoons flour
- 1 cup whipping cream
- 5 egg yolks
- 8 ounces goat cheese, crumbled
    Salt, pepper, nutmeg, cayenne, to taste
- 1 teaspoon thyme
- 1 tablespoon fresh chives
- 5 to 7 egg whites (depending on how fluffy a soufflé you like)

Make a roux by melting the butter and slowly stirring in the flour. Continue to cook over low heat until flour is cooked, but not browned. Turn down heat, and gradually stir in whipping cream and half the goat cheese. Remove from heat and slowly add the beaten egg yolks, stirring after each small addition. Add the remaining goat cheese, and salt, pepper, nutmeg, and cayenne to taste. Add thyme and chives.

Beat egg whites until stiff. Add a quarter of the egg whites to the cheese mixture, and stir in to lighten mixture. Add the rest of the egg whites at one time and fold into the cheese mixture, being careful not to deflate the egg whites.

Pour into a buttered 1½ quart soufflé dish and bake in a preheated 350° oven for 30 to 40 minutes until puffed and golden. Soufflé should be almost gooey inside.

Serve with a light tomato sauce over each portion.

Serves 4 to 6

Try with: Chardonnay, Merlot

"The nice thing about this recipe is that it is very good with a full Chardonnay, as well as being able to stand up to reds. At a dinner for Matanzas Creek, Jeremiah Tower prepared a fabulous goat cheese soufflé that flattered the wine served with it to such an extent that I had never tasted our own wine and enjoyed it that fully before!"

FRESH ARTICHOKE FRITTATA   Shown & Sons Vineyards
To serve hot or cold

> 3 or 4 large artichokes, cooked
> 1 onion, finely chopped
> 2 cloves garlic, minced
> ½ cup fresh parsley, chopped
>   Olive oil
> 8 eggs, beaten well
> 2 slices white bread
> ½ cup half-and-half
> ½ cup Parmesan cheese, grated
> 1 teaspoon Italian seasoning
>   Salt and pepper to taste
>   Paprika

Scrape each artichoke leaf to remove "meat". Discard stripped leaves. Chop heart. Set aside.

Sauté onion, garlic and parsley until onion is translucent and tender. Combine with artichoke. Set aside.

Blend beaten eggs with bread, cheese and seasonings. Combine thoroughly with artichoke mixture. Pour all into lightly buttered 13x9x2-inch baking dish. Sprinkle with paprika.

Bake 30 minutes at 350°. Slice into large squares for main dish, or 2-inch squares for appetizer.

Serves 8 as main dish, more as an appetizer

Try with: Johannisberg Riesling

"This also holds its own with Cabernet Sauvignon as a side dish with rich pasta. To make it suitable for full-bodied Cabernet, add more garlic and onion, and a sprig or two of fresh basil."

ZUCCHINI TORTA   Sebastiani Vineyards

First, prepare:

Cheese Anise Pastry

1¼ cups flour
½ teaspoon salt
½ teaspoon anise seeds, crushed
½ cup butter or margarine
½ cup cheddar cheese, grated

Stir the salt and anise seeds into flour. Add butter and cheese
and work into flour with food processor or fingers, mixing
well to form dough. Pat in an even layer over the bottom and
one inch up the sides of an 8-inch spring form pan.

And then make ...

Zucchini Filling

8 slices bacon
2 tablespoons bacon drippings
2 cups zucchini, thinly sliced
½ cup onion, finely chopped
2 teaspoons garlic, minced
1 cup sour cream
6 eggs
1 teaspoon salt
2 cups rice, cooked in half Chenin Blanc and half water
1 cup grated cheddar cheese

Cook bacon in large skillet until crisp. Drain, reserving 2
tablespoons fat. Crumble bacon and set aside. Heat reserved
drippings in skillet, add zucchini, onion and garlic and cook
10 minutes, stirring occasionally.

Beat eggs in large bowl. Add sour cream, salt, cooked rice,
cheese, vegetable mixture and crumbled bacon. Turn into
pastry shell and smooth the top. Bake at 350° about 55
minutes, or until golden brown and set. Let stand at least five
minutes, then loosen the edges and remove sides of the pan.
Cut into wedges to serve warm or cold.

Serves 8

RED PEPPER TART

Inglenook Vineyards
Barbara Lang

This dish requires a genuinely flaky crust. Make your own, or use partially baked pastry crust from the supermarket. You will need enough dough to cover a 12-inch tart pan one-eighths inch thick. For a flaky crust, be sure the butter or shortening pieces never become smaller than lima beans when incorporated into the flour.

Roll dough out and place in tart pan. Crimp edges. Refrigerate for at least an hour to avoid shrinkage while baking.

Preheat oven to 400°. Over sheet of foil placed on pastry dough, heap dried beans or raw rice (to prevent dough's bubbling and shifting) and bake for 10 minutes. Remove the foil and beans and bake dough another 5 minutes. Remove from oven. If there are any gaps in crust, "mend" by filling in with any kind of mild grated cheese. Return to oven for three minutes for cheese to melt and seal crust.

Set aside to cool on rack. Lower oven temperature to 375°.

Filling

- 2 sweet red bell peppers. If not available, use green bell peppers plus ¼ cup of canned sliced pimientos.
- 4 tablespoons butter
- 2 cloves garlic, minced
- 1 onion, thinly sliced
- ¼ cup chopped parsley
- 2 eggs, slightly beaten
- ¾ cup whipping cream
- 4 ounces goat cheese
- ¾ cup ricotta
- ½ teaspoon salt
- ¼ teaspoon freshly ground black pepper

Place peppers over high fire on gas burner or broil in electric stove, turning periodically until charred all over. Place peppers in brown paper bag, roll shut for about ten minutes until they steam enough to peel easily. Remove from bag and scrape off charred skin. Slice into ¼-inch strips and set aside.

Melt butter in small saucepan, add garlic and cook gently over low heat. Add onions and cook until translucent. Stir in parsley. Remove from heat and set aside.

In large mixing bowl, add eggs, cream, goat cheese, ricotta, salt and pepper. Stir until well blended. (To incorporate, mash goat cheese against mixing bowl with back of wooden spoon.) Stir in onion-garlic-parsley mixture. Pour into baked crust in pie pan and place on baking sheet to capture any escaping fluid. Decorate top in spiral design with the sliced peppers.

Bake at 375° for 30 minutes until tart sets and is light brown in color.

Serves 6 as a main course or 8 to 10 as a first course

Try with: Fumé Blanc

GARDEN VARIETY PITA SANDWICH   Gundlach-Bundschu Winery

2 tablespoons olive oil
1 clove garlic, grated
1 medium onion, chopped
1 small potato, sliced thin
2 or 3 medium zucchini, sliced thin
12 cherry tomatoes
½ pound tofu (bean curd) cut into 1-inch cubes
¼ pound hard jack cheese, grated
½ cup Riesling
   Pinch fresh parsley, minced
   Pinch dried basil or tarragon
   Sour cream (optional)

Sauté garlic and onion in oil. Add potato slices, simmer two minutes. Add zucchini, simmer one minute. Add tofu, Riesling, grated cheese, cherry tomatoes, and herbs. Simmer until all vegetables are cooked to your liking.

Warm pita bread and cut in half. Fill with the vegetable mixture. Add more grated cheese and/or a dollop of sour cream.

Try with: Riesling, Kleinberger

RISOTTO CON FONDUTA Y ASPARAGI

Sebastiani Vineyards

3 cups cooked moist white rice, cooked half in water and half in Chenin Blanc
1 pound asparagus, cooked al dente and cut into ½ inch pieces
8 ounces Fontina cheese
½ cup half & half
2 teaspoons flour
  Dash white pepper
3 egg yolks, slightly beaten
2 tablespoons butter, cut in small pieces

Grate cheese and place in shallow bowl with ¼ cup half-and-half. Cover and let stand for 30 minutes. Blend flour and pepper with egg yolks and the remaining ¼ cup half & half. Cook in the top of a double boiler (water should not touch the underside of the upper portion of the pot). Stir constantly over low heat until thickened and smooth. Add cheese, continuing to simmer until melted. Stir in butter until melted. Combine asparagus bits, rice and cheese sauce and serve hot.

Serves 8

Try with: Vin Rosé, Fumé Blanc, Chenin Blanc, Eye of the Swan

Pasta

CORNISH GAME HEN   **Vose Vineyards**

½ bottle (750-ml) Fumé Blanc
3 Cornish game hens, semi-defrosted for easy slicing
1 whole bulb garlic, broken into cloves
2 cups flour, approximately
1 teaspoon sage
1 teaspoon lemon pepper
Seasoned salt to taste (Lawry's, if available)
¼ teaspoon red chili pepper
1 pint half & half
2 red tomatoes, cut in quarters
2 green tomatoes (tomatillos), cut in quarters
24 Greek olives
¼ cup olive oil

Place flour, dried herbs, salt and pepper in large paper bag. Shake vigorously and set aside.

Remove giblets, and slice semi-defrosted game hens in half. Rub halves with olive oil. Place in paper sack with herbs and flour and shake until coated well.

Remove hen halves from sack and place in lightly greased roasting pan, and pour the wine over them. Peel garlic and submerge all cloves, whole, in the wine. Arrange tomato quarters around the hens, and then the olives.

Bake in 450° oven for 45 minutes, or until brown and crisp on the outside. Just before serving, stir in the half & half. If you prefer a thicker sauce, blend ½ cup of herb-flour mixture with ½ cup cold water. Stir small amounts of this very slowly into the sauce, tasting after each addition while adjusting sauce.

Arrange your favorite pasta, cooked al dente, on serving platter with sauce over it.

Serves 6

Try with: Fumé Blanc

LINGUINI TOMASSO   **Sterling Vineyards**

Sauce

¼ stick butter
¼ cup olive oil
1 tablespoon flour
⅓ cup chicken broth
⅔ cup white wine
1 garlic clove, minced
1 tablespoon parsley, chopped
2-3 tablespoons lemon juice
Salt and pepper
2 cans (14-ounce) artichoke hearts, drained and chopped
2 tablespoons grated Parmesan cheese
2 teaspoons capers, rinsed and drained
1 tablespoon butter, softened
2 tablespoons olive oil
Linguini, cooked al dente and drained

In large saucepan with cover melt butter with oil over medium heat. Add flour and stir until smooth (3 minutes). Blend in broth and wine and stir until thick. Reduce heat to low.

Add the next four ingredients. Cook 5 minutes, stirring constantly.

Blend in artichokes, cheese, and capers. Cover and simmer about 8 minutes.

Melt remaining butter in large skillet and stir in remaining oil, cheese, and salt. Add linguini and toss.

Arrange pasta on heated platter and pour the sauce over it.

Try with: Sauvignon Blanc, Chardonnay

LINGUINI AL TONNO   Charles Krug Winery

    3 tablespoons olive oil
    1 medium onion, sliced
    1 7-ounce can tuna
    1 can tomato paste
1½ to 2 cups lukewarm water
    3 or 4 fillets of anchovies, minced
       Salt and pepper to taste
    2 to 3 cloves garlic, minced (optional)

Sauté onion in oil until transparent, adding garlic slightly later, as it burns easily. In separate bowl with heavy spoon, flake and shred tuna as fine as possible. Add tuna to onion and garlic and simmer 5 minutes, stirring often to prevent tuna from forming into lumps. Dilute tomato paste with lukewarm water and add it along with the anchovies to the above mixture. Simmer about 15 minutes, stirring often.

Serve over cooked linguini or spaghetti.

Serves 4 to 6

Try with: Gamay Beaujolais, Zinfandel

PASTA SAUCES   Harvey Steiman

To discover how various food flavors can be enhanced by different wines, and vice versa, Louis P. Martini suggests a Pasta Party. The host is responsible for one bottle of wine and and for the cooked spaghetti or fettucini, and each guest for a different wine and a pasta sauce that might be compatible.

The following recipes for a pasta party are the inventions of Harvey Steiman, Food & Wine Editor of the *San Francisco Examiner*.

Garlic Herb Butter

Place 6 tablespoons butter in a cold skillet with a branch of rosemary and 2 cloves garlic cut in half lengthwise. Melt butter slowly. When butter is melted, remove the rosemary and garlic. Toss the pasta with melted butter before serving.

Sauce Alfredo

In large skillet bring 6 tablespoons butter and 1 cup whipping cream slowly to boil, and let boil for one minute. Remove from heat. Beat in 3 eggs and ½ cup grated Parmesan cheese. Serve with additional grated cheese.

Anchovy-Walnut Sauce

Melt 1½ sticks butter in a saucepan over low heat. Add 1 teaspoon finely chopped garlic, 1 tablespoon finely chopped fresh basil, and 6 ounces ground or chopped walnuts and cook the mixture for a few minutes. Add 2 or 3 mashed anchovy fillets and 1 cup whipping cream. Simmer the mixture for 10 minutes. Stir in ½ cup grated Parmesan cheese and additional cream if necessary to make a thick but spoonable sauce.

Red Clam Sauce

In large skillet, sauté 1 teaspoon finely chopped garlic in 3 tablespoons olive oil until very lightly browned. Add 1 tablespoon chopped parsley, a few grinds of black pepper, a pinch oregano, and 1 cup peeled Italian tomatoes, drained and chopped. Cook mixture 10 minutes, then add 3 dozen clams. Cook clams in sauce until they open wide and serve immediately.

Pesto-Potato Sauce

A variation on a classic originated by Alfredo Viazzi.

Cut ¾ pound peeled boiling potatoes into ½-inch cubes. Boil potatoes in lightly salted water until tender. Drain well and sauté in 2 tablespoons butter for 10 minutes. Add 1 cup pesto sauce [see index] and half a cup of the water that pasta was boiled in. Serve with grated Pecorino cheese.

SPAGHETTINI PRIMAVERA
Louis M. Martini

- 1 pound hot Italian sausage
- 4 tablespoons olive oil
- 2 cloves garlic, finely minced
- 1 28-ounce can Italian plum tomatoes, drained and chopped
- 1 cup parsley, finely chopped
- 1 sprig fresh oregano or 1 teaspoon dried
  Salt, freshly ground black pepper
- 1 pound dried Italian spaghettini
- ½ pound Chinese (snow) peas, strings removed and chilled in ice water
- ½ pound young zucchini, thinly sliced
- 3 red bell peppers, thinly sliced
- ¼ cup fresh basil, chopped
- ¾ cup grated Parmesan cheese

Cover sausages with water and boil until cooked, about 30 minutes. Remove from heat, peel, and cut in thin slices. Heat 2 tablespoons olive oil in heavy skillet over medium heat. Add sausage and brown. Remove sausage from skillet and discard all but 2 tablespoons of the accumulated fat.

Add garlic and sauté until transparent, but do not brown. Add tomatoes, parsley, oregano, salt and pepper. Cover and simmer gently for 15 minutes, stirring from time to time to prevent burning or sticking. Add a little water if it gets too dry. Remove from heat, add sausage, and cover to keep mixture warm. While sauce is cooking, cook spaghettini according to directions.

Meanwhile, in another skillet, add the remaining 2 tablespoons oil and heat to medium high. Dry snow peas on paper towels. Add zucchini and red bell peppers to skillet and sauté for a few minutes. Then add snow peas and cook until they turn bright green. Add vegetables to sauce.

Toss thoroughly with pasta and fresh basil. Sprinkle with parsley and Parmesan to serve.

Serves 4 to 6

Try with: Cabernet Sauvignon, Merlot

SEAFOOD PASTA

Inglenook Vineyards
Barbara Lang

Court Bouillon

Simmer the following ingredients in a large stockpot:

  1 onion, sliced
  1 carrot, coarsely chopped
  2 celery stalks, coarsely chopped
  6 sprigs parsley
  1 teaspoon dried thyme, or 2 sprigs fresh
  1 teaspoon dried dill weed, or 1 tablespoon fresh
  1 bay leaf
  4 to 6 whole peppercorns
  6 cups water
  2 cups dry white wine

Add shells (only) of shrimp and bring liquid to boil. Lower heat and simmer for 30 minutes. Strain court bouillon and return it to stockpot. Reduce liquid by simmering until it covers just about an inch of the stockpot. Seafood will be added later to be steamed, *not* poached.

Pasta: 6 ounces green spinach pasta, barely cooked al dente, strained and put in a large bowl of cold water.

Sauce: 2 tablespoons unsalted butter
    1 tablespoon shallots, minced
    1½ cups whipping cream
    ½ teaspoon salt
    Pinch of white pepper
    1 teaspoon dried dill weed, or 1 tablespoon fresh

Sauté shallots in melted butter over low to medium heat for 5 minutes, stirring occasionally. Add cream and raise heat to reduce liquid to ¾ cup, being very careful that cream does not boil over. Add 3 tablespoons of strained court bouillon, salt, pepper, and dill. Remove from heat and set aside.

Seafood: 8 clams, scrubbed
    8 mussels, scrubbed
    8 medium or jumbo shrimp, peeled and deveined (use shells in court bouillon)

Heat court bouillon until simmering. Add the clams, cover stockpot and steam for 2 minutes. Then add the mussels, cover, and steam for 1 minute. Add the shrimp, cover, and steam for 4 minutes, or until the shrimp is bright pink and shells of the clams and mussels have opened. Turn heat off.

Gently reheat the dill-cream sauce.

Reheat pasta cooking water to simmering, add pasta and cook until done (about a minute). Strain and return pasta to empty, heated pasta pot. Pour about ¼ cup of the sauce over pasta and thoroughly toss.

Serve pasta on heated plates and top with 2 shrimp, 2 mussels, and 2 clams each. Pour sauce over each. Garnish with sprig of fresh dill or snip of parsley.

Serves 4

Try with: Chardonnay

CLAM PASTA   **Louis M. Martini**

2 tablespoons butter
2 tablespoons flour
1 or 2 cloves garlic, minced
1½ cups half & half
1 10-ounce can whole baby clams, with juice reserved
¼ teaspoon thyme
Salt and white pepper, to taste
8 ounces dried pasta, cooked
2 pounds freshly steamed clams (optional)
Parmesan cheese

Drain clams and reserve liquid. In a medium saucepan melt butter and garlic, and sauté briefly. Do not allow to color. Add flour and cook for 2 minutes. Whisk in half & half, reserved clam juice and cook until sauce thickens. Season with thyme, salt and white pepper. Remove sauce from heat and add clams. Cook the pasta and toss with sauce. Garnish with steamed clams, if desired, and serve with Parmesan cheese.

Serves 6 as a first course, 4 as an entrée

Side Dishes

BAJA BANANAS   Sebastiani Vineyards

4 large, firm bananas
½ cup Gewurztraminer
¼ cup butter or margarine
1 teaspoon curry powder
2 tablespoons brown sugar

Cut bananas in half lengthwise, then in half crosswise. Soak in Gewurztraminer for 10 minutes.

Meanwhile, melt butter in a shallow baking dish in preheated 350° oven. Stir in the curry powder and brown sugar. Dip the banana pieces in the mixture, turning to coat well, and bake in the same baking dish about 15 minutes.

Serves 6 to 8 as accompaniment to any plain meat, roast, fish, or chicken.

CARROT SALAD   Richard Alexei
Monticello Cellars

1 pound fresh carrots, peeled and shredded with grater or
   food processor
1 green onion, chopped
3 to 4 fresh sprigs Italian parsley, chopped
1 small sprig oregano or marjoram, chopped
¼ cup Napa Valley Vinaigrette
   Freshly ground black pepper
   Salt to taste

Combine carrots, onion, herbs, vinaigrette, and pepper and salt to taste. Refrigerate at least two hours before serving.

Serves 6

GEWURZTRAMINER BRAISED RICE

Hacienda Wine Cellars

   1 cup white rice
   1 cup dry Gewurztraminer
   1 cup chicken stock
   ½ cup finely chopped shallots
   2 to 4 tablespoons unsalted butter
      Bouquet garni — a pinch each of tarragon and thyme
         plus ⅓ crushed bay leaf and a sprig of fresh parsley

Preheat oven to 350°.

Melt butter in a heavy saucepan or casserole that has an ovenproof lid. Add shallots and sauté until soft. Add rice and stir until cooked to a milky appearance. Meanwhile, have the combined Gewurztraminer and stock brought to a boil in a separate pan. Add the boiling liquid to the rice mixture as soon as it is cooked properly, as above. Add bouquet garni, cover, and place in preheated oven. Rice should cook in simmering liquid about 20 minutes. When done, discard bouquet garni and fluff the rice with a fork.

Serves 4 as "a subtle side dish for all sorts of well-spiced main dishes."

Try with: Gewurztraminer

Napa Valley Vinaigrette

In blender combine:

   1 cup red wine vinegar
   1 heaping teaspoon salt
   ½ teaspoon freshly ground black pepper
   2 teaspoons Dijon-style mustard

Process until smooth. Slowly add 1½ cups green, fruity olive oil and 2 cups bland salad oil to form a smooth emulsion. Transfer to a jar. Shake thoroughly before using.

RICOTTA STUFFED SQUASH FLOWERS
Sebastiani Vineyards

Approximately 12 medium squash flowers (zucchini or
    any other), freshly picked and carefully rinsed in cold
    water
  1 pound ricotta cheese
  1 onion, chopped
  ½ cup toasted almonds, finely chopped
  ½ cup Italian Asiago or Parmesan cheese, grated
  ½ teaspoon ground pepper
  1 teaspoon seasoning salt
  2 tablespoons fresh minced basil or 1 teaspoon dried
  2 tablespoons parsley

Proportions will vary according to number and size of
flowers. Use pastry tube to stuff flowers — but don't overfill.
Filling should be used at room temperature. Be careful not to
let filling ooze out of flowers.

Drizzle 1 teaspoon melted butter over flowers and cook in
microwave on medium for 3 minutes, or in regular oven at
350° for 15 minutes.

ROAST GARLIC & NEW POTATO SALAD
Sterling Vineyards

  2 full heads of garlic
  ¼ cup olive oil
  ¼ cup butter
  ¼ cup Sauvignon Blanc
  2 pounds small red potatoes
    Foil

Preheat oven 325°. Parboil potatoes with skins on for ten
minutes. Peel garlic. Melt butter and oil in oven in a 9 x
13-inch pan. Remove pan from oven and stir in wine. Add
potatoes and garlic, cover pan tightly with foil and return to
oven. Baste every 15 minutes until fork-tender. Serve at room
temperature.

Serves 8

Desserts

FRUIT COMPOTE
Rutherford Hill Winery

In a ceramic or glass serving bowl combine as many as possible of the following fruits, peeled as necessary and cut into bite-size pieces:

Oranges, Apples, Pears, Grapes, Fresh Pineapple, Melon, Berries

Pour the following **Marinade** over the fruit:

1 cup Pinot Noir or Gerwurztraminer
1 tablespoon grated fresh ginger
1 tablespoon grated orange rind
¼ cup orange flavored liqueur (Grand Marnier or Triple Sec)

Refrigerate for at least half an hour before serving.

If fruit is marinated per recipe and skewered and broiled until warmed through, this compote becomes Kebobs, to accompany meat or to serve with brunch.

SHERRY CREAM FOR FRESH FRUIT
Louis M. Martini

To prepare and chill up to 3 hours before serving

1 cup sour cream
3 tablespoons soft brown sugar
3 tablespoons Cream Sherry
2 cups fresh blueberries
2 cups fresh nectarines, sliced

Mix first three ingredients together until creamy and smooth. This may be prepared ahead and refrigerated until ready to use.

Stir in fruit — as above or in any other fresh fruit combination desired. Be sure that all cut fruit is well coated so it will not darken.

APRICOT BAVAROIS
Chateau St. Jean
Linda Hagen

   6 egg yolks
12 ounces dried apricots (12 reserved for garnish)
   6 ounces apricot nectar
¾ cup sugar
   2 teaspoons cornstarch
1½ cup warm milk
   2 envelopes unflavored gelatin
   6 egg whites
   2 tablespoons sugar
   1 cup whipping cream
   3 tablespoons Grand Marnier
   2 tablespoons sugar

Purée apricots and nectar. Beat egg yolks. Add sugar, milk, gelatin and cornstarch. Blend with apricot purée. Heat — but do not boil — until mixture coats spoon. Cool for half an hour.

Beat egg whites and sugar. Blend into apricot mixture. Chill for half an hour.

Whip cream, Grand Marnier and sugar. Blend into apricot mixture. Pour into lightly oiled half-cup soufflé dishes or small ramekins. Chill. Unmold to serve, and garnish as below.

Garnish

   1 cup whipping cream
   3 tablespoons Grand Marnier
   2 tablespoons sugar
12 dried apricots (reconstituted and reserved)
12 fresh mint leaves

Whip cream, Grand Marnier and sugar. Spoon onto unmolded Apricot Bavarois, and garnish with whole apricot and mint leaf.

Serves 12

Try with: Late Harvest Johannisberg Riesling, Late Harvest Gewurztraminer

LILA'S COOL DESSERT   Adler Fels

Basic Dessert Crepes

   1½ cups flour
   1 tablespoon sugar
   3 eggs
   1½ cups milk
      Pinch of salt
   3 tablespoons melted butter

Place all ingredients in blender and beat well. Let batter stand one hour or longer before sautéing crepes in butter, turning once. Set crepes aside until filling is prepared. This batter freezes well.

Filling

   8 ounces non-dairy whipped topping, such as Cool Whip
   2 cans chocolate pudding (10 ounces)
   1 cup chopped walnuts
   1 bottle chocolate or chocolate mint ice cream topping
      (Magic Shell)
      Whipping cream
   6 maraschino cherries, halved

Place whipped topping in a large bowl and allow to soften. Add pudding and mix together. Add ¾ cup chopped walnuts. Mix, cover, and put in freezer until firm — 2 to 4 hours.

Place approximately 3 heaping teaspoonfuls across center of crepe. Fold one side of crepe over filling, and then the other, and place on cookie sheet to store. When crepes are filled, cover with plastic wrap and freeze. This can be done up to 24 hours before serving.

To serve, place on dessert dishes. Decorate with remaining nuts, cherry halves and chocolate topping, to which has been added a dash of cream. This recipe may be doubled.

Try with: Champagne

GOAT CHEESE ICE CREAM   Scottie McKinney

  1 cup California Chevre plain fromage blanc, Laura
    Chenel's
  1 cup sugar
  1 cup whipping cream
  4 egg yolks

Combine all ingredients and place in ice cream freezer.
Process according to manufacturer's directions.

Serves 4 to 6

Try with: Gewurztraminer

CHERRIES JUBILEE   The Christian Brothers

Have serving dishes ready with scoops of vanilla ice cream.

Put ¾ cup red currant jelly into chafing dish or top of double
boiler over low heat.

Drain one No. 2-½ can (3-½ cups) pitted red cherries and add
to jelly, until cherries are heated and jelly is melted.

Measure ½ cup brandy into warmed metal ladle. Pour into
center of cherries and heat without stirring. When heated,
light with taper and ladle over ice cream while flaming.

For dramatic effect, dim the lights just before lighting the
brandy, and if a chafing dish is available, use it for esthetic
appeal. As with any dish where flame is involved, the usual
preliminary precautions — a bottle of water on standby, or
baking soda in the vicinity — are advised.

Serves 6

POACHED PEARS   Robert Pecota Winery

    3 pears cut in half with core removed
2½ cups apple juice
    1 pomegranate
    10 to 12 coriander seeds
    1 teaspoon orange zest (rind)

Cut pomegranate in half, saving some seeds for garnish, and squeezing juice from the remainder into a shallow pan (2-inch sides) that will hold poaching liquid and the pears to be added. Add apple juice and coriander seeds and boil gently for 5 minutes. Add pears and simmer gently, uncovered, until tender (about 5 more minutes).

Garnish with pomegranate seeds and curled strips of orange zest.

Serve chilled or at room temperature.

Serves 6.

Try with: Muscato di Andrea

RHINE FARM PUDDING   Buena Vista Vineyards
Courtesy of Mrs. Frank H. Bartholomew

    5 eggs, separated
    1 cup plus 2 tablespoons granulated sugar
      Juice and grated peel of 1 lemon
    1 envelope unflavored gelatin
    ¼ cup Johannisberger Riesling or other white dinner wine,
      heated

Combine egg yolks, sugar, lemon juice and grated lemon peel; beat for 10 minutes. Soften gelatin in cold water; dissolve in hot wine. Add slowly to egg mixture. Beat egg whites until stiff and fold into gelatin mixture. Chill. Serve mounded high in parfait or sherbet glasses, and garnished with a lemon leaf and blossom if available.

Try with: Johannisberg Riesling

SPIRITED HOLIDAY FRUIT CAKE   The Christian Brothers

Marinate the fruits for a month or more, and bake this at least two weeks before serving.

> 1½ cups shelled pecans, broken in pieces
> ¾ pound candied grapefruit strips, cut into pieces
> 1 pound candied pineapple slices, cut into pieces
> 1 pound candied citron, cut into pieces
> ¾ pound candied orange peel, cut into pieces
> 1½ pounds seedless dates, cut in thirds
> 1 cup dark seedless raisins
> ¾ pound glacé red cherries, half of them left whole, for garnish, the remainder cut in half
> 2 cups Brandy
> 1 cup Dry Sherry

Layer the fruits and nuts in a stone crock or large glass container with cover and add the brandy and sherry. Cover with damp cloth and then with lid, or mold heavy aluminum foil over top.

Each week remove cover and stir well. To properly stir, you may need to empty fruit and liquids into a bowl and then return them afterward to crock. The usual long aging period for the cake is eliminated when the fruit is marinated ahead.

• • •

The following recipe fills two loaf pans and one medium size tube pan. You may use any size container, but remember that the deeper pans will take longer to bake, and the slices may need to be cut further to serve.

Prepare cake pans the evening before baking by lining with two thicknesses of brown paper well-greased with melted vegetable shortening.

Cake

> 1 pound butter, softened
> 2 cups granulated sugar
> 1 dozen fresh eggs, slightly beaten
> 4½ cups sifted all-purpose flour
> ½ teaspoon salt
> 1 teaspoon baking powder
> ¼ teaspoon ground mace
> ¼ teaspoon ground cloves
> ½ teaspoon grated nutmeg
> ½ teaspoon cinnamon

Cream butter in electric mixer until light, and slowly add sugar, beating constantly. Add eggs and beat until well blended, keeping mixture light. Sift flour with salt, baking powder and spices, and slowly add to mixture until blended together.

Add the marinated fruit and liquid and mix together with the cake batter until mixing spoon is coated. Fill prepared pans almost full, pressing down with back of spoon.

Bake at 275° about 2 hours and 40 minutes. Should browning occur too soon, loosely cover each cake with aluminum foil. Test for doneness by inserting food pick just off center; if it comes out clean, the cake is done.

To Decorate

> ½ cup white corn syrup
> Walnut halves or other nuts
> Reserved cherry halves
> Cheesecloth wet with brandy

Heat syrup until boiling. When cool, dip cherries and nuts in syrup and stick on cakes in a decorative pattern. When fruit is set, wrap cake in cheesecloth wet with brandy. Wrap in foil and store in refrigerator until ready to serve.

Try with: Cream Sherry

WALNUT TART

Richard Alexei
Monticello Cellars

A food processor is recommended for this tart, which is best if made the same day it is to be served.

Crust

If prepared in food processor, use steel blade.

¼ pound sweet butter, chilled and cut into pieces.
1½ cups flour
¼ cup sugar
2 egg yolks

Combine butter, flour and sugar until mixture resembles fine oatmeal. Add yolks and blend until incorporated. Squeeze dough. Transfer to an 11-inch tart pan with removable bottom. Press dough evenly on sides and bottom. Prick with fork. Chill until filling is ready to use.

Filling:

1 egg
1 cup walnut meats
½ cup heavy cream
¼ cup packed light brown sugar
1-inch piece ginger root, peeled

Combine the above in a food processor, and process until puréed.

Pour into pastry shell and bake in 350° oven for 20 minutes.

Meanwhile, prepare **Topping:**

¼ cup light brown sugar
2 tablespoons Madeira or Sherry
1 cup walnut halves

Combine sugar and wine in saucepan. Bring to boil and boil for a few seconds, stirring until sugar is completely dissolved.

Arrange walnut halves over top of partially baked tart, pressing in slightly. Dribble wine-sugar glaze evenly over nuts. Return tart to oven and bake about 35 minutes longer, or until filling puffs, then sinks, and crust is a light golden brown. Let cool for five minutes. Remove from pan.

Serves 8

LIME SOUFFLÉ TART
Beringer Vineyards

California Culinary Academy Scholarship Winner

10-inch unbaked sweet pastry crust
¾ cup sugar
4 egg yolks
   Grated rind of 3 limes
3 tablespoons lime juice
4 egg whites
   Pinch of salt
¼ to ⅓ cup powdered sugar

Beat egg yolks and ½ cup sugar until light and fluffy enough to leave a track when a spoon is pulled through it. Mix in the rind and juice.

Cook over a double boiler, stirring constantly, until mixture is thick and hot to the touch, being very careful not to scramble the eggs. Remove from heat.

Beat the whites and salt until foamy. Slowly add ¼ cup of the powdered sugar and whip until whites retain a stiff peak.

With a rubber spatula, gently fold the egg whites into the warm lime mixture. Pour into crust.

Bake at 325° for 25 minutes. The mixture will rise and be lightly browned. Sprinkle with the remaining powdered sugar and bake for 5 more minutes.

Serves 10 to 12

Try with: Late Harvest Johannisberg Riesling

FRUIT COMPOTE
The Christian Brothers

Brother Timothy, Cellarmaster

A simple dessert to serve with cookies.
"The sweetness of our Chateau La Salle precludes it from being acceptable with something like a steak or with very many different foods at the dinner table, but it goes great with desserts of all kinds. You can splash it over fruit — strawberries or peaches — and make a nice dessert."

STRAWBERRIES WITH DOUBLE CREAM

Robert Mondavi Winery

    3 egg yolks
    ¼ cup sugar
    ¼ teaspoon vanilla
    1½ tablespoons cornstarch
    ¾ cup milk, scalded
    2 pints strawberries, hulled
    ½ cup almond flavored liqueur (Amaretto)
    1 cup heavy cream, whipped

In a small pan mix yolks, sugar and vanilla. Stir in cornstarch; add milk gradually. Cook over medium heat, stirring constantly until very thick (2 or 3 minutes). Remove this custard to a bowl, cover and refrigerate.

Combine strawberries and liqueur. Cover and refrigerate for approximately two hours.

Stir half the whipped cream into custard. Gently fold in remaining cream so that airiness is maintained. Cover and refrigerate.

To serve, spoon strawberries with liqueur into dessert bowls. Top with generous spoonfuls of the custard double cream.

Serves 6 to 8

Try with: Late Harvest Johannisberg Riesling

"This simple but elegant dessert is also delicious prepared with peeled, sliced nectarines or peaches."

LILA'S EASY DESSERT

Adler Fels

- Flour Tortilla, 1 per serving
- Butter
- Banana
- Brown Sugar
- Cinnamon
- Whipped cream or ice cream garnish

Spray or butter a cookie sheet. Butter both sides of tortilla. Place a banana, cut to size, in center. Sprinkle a dessert spoon or more of sugar over banana and tortilla. Sprinkle cinnamon on top. Roll and place seam side down. Sprinkle small amount of cinnamon on top.

Preheat oven to 400°. Bake until brown and crisp. Serve with whipped cream or ice cream.

This can also be served plain for breakfast.

Try with: Johannisberg Riesling, Gewurztraminer

ITALIAN CHOCOLATE LACE COOKIES

Sebastiani Vineyards

- 1 cup flour
- 1 cup finely chopped pecans
- ½ cup corn syrup
- ¼ cup shortening
- ¼ cup butter
- ⅓ cup brown sugar
- 1 12-ounce package chocolate chips

Blend flour and nuts and set aside. Bring corn syrup, shortening and sugar to boil over medium heat, stirring constantly. Remove from heat and gradually stir in flour and nuts. Drop by tablespoon onto lightly greased baking sheet. Bake at 375° for 6 to 8 minutes. Let stand 5 minutes before removing from baking sheet. As batter cools, either reheat slightly, or bake cookies 1 additional minute.

Place chocolate chips in double boiler over hot water and stir. When partially melted, remove from the hot water and stir until melted. Then spread on bottom of each cooled cookie. Set cookies upside down until chocolate has set and dried.

Makes 10 to 12 3-inch cookies

SILVER PIE   Charles Krug Winery

½ package gelatin
½ cup water
4 egg yolks, beaten well
½ cup sugar
5 tablespoons lemon juice
Grated rind of 1 lemon
4 egg whites
⅓ cup sugar
1 baked pie shell
Whipped cream

Soak gelatin in water. Beat egg yolks with ½ cup sugar. Add lemon juice and rind and cook in top of double boiler until thick. Stir in gelatin. Cool.

Beat egg whites with ⅓ cup sugar until stiff and fold into first mixture.

Pour into baked pie shell and chill. Top with whipped cream.

Serves 6 to 8

Try with: Muscat Canelli

ZABAGLIONE   Louis M. Martini

For each person:

1 tablespoon Cream Sherry
1 tablespoon powdered sugar
1 egg yolk
Nutmeg, freshly grated

Mix the above in the top of a double boiler (preferably heavyweight). Over simmering water, never allowing the water to touch the bottom of the pan, beat with an electric hand beater until thick and fluffy — ten minutes or so. Serve immediately in small glasses with grated nutmeg on top.

Crisp, plain butter or walnut cookies, Italian anise bars, or lady fingers make a nice accompaniment.

WHITE CHOCOLATE GANACHE   Scottie McKinney

   1 pound white chocolate (in block form)
   ½ cup sweet butter, softened to room temperature
   2 egg yolks
   2 tablespoons cream
   3 tablespoons late harvest Riesling (room temperature)
     Raspberry Sauce, recipe below

Melt chocolate in top of double boiler. Remove from heat.
Add butter, egg yolks, cream, and wine, stirring with whisk
until all ingredients are incorporated into the white chocolate
(liquid will separate initially). Pour into lightly oiled individual molds. Chill several hours or overnight. Unmold and
serve with Raspberry Sauce. (This may also be chilled in a
large bowl and served into dishes with ice cream scoop or
large serving spoon.)

Raspberry Sauce

   2 cups fresh or frozen raspberries
   1 tablespoon sugar
   1 tablespoon late harvest Riesling

Combine all ingredients in food processor or blender until
smooth.

Serves 6 to 8

Try with: Sparkling Blanc de Noir, Champagne (medium dry)

CREAMY COLD ZABAGLIONE   Louis M. Martini

This cold version may be made as much as 2 or 3 hours before
serving and still retain the flavor of the Cream Sherry. Make
Zabaglione as in previous recipe, for six people. Beat ½ pint
of heavy whipping cream until very stiff. Fold the cream into
the freshly made Zabaglione, and turn into individual serving
dishes or a single glass serving bowl. Chill until ready to serve
with a little grated nutmeg on top.

Serves 8

Index

CONTRIBUTORS

WINES